Global Citizenship for
Young Children

OXFORD BROOKES
UNIVERSITY
LIBRARY

A Lucky Duck Book

00 812197 OX T

Referenced ✓

Global Citizenship for Young Children

Margaret Collins

Illustrations by Philippa Drakeford

Los Angeles • London • New Delhi • Singapore

© Margaret Collins 2008
Illustrations © Philippa Drakeford 2008

First published 2008

Apart from any fair dealing for the purposes of research or private
study, or criticism or review, as permitted under the Copyright,
Designs and Patents Act, 1988, this publication may be reproduced,
stored or transmitted in any form, or by any means, only with the
prior permission in writing of the publishers, or in the case of
reprographic reproduction, in accordance with the terms of licences
issued by the Copyright Licensing Agency. Enquiries concerning
reproduction outside those terms should be sent to the publishers.

The right of the Author to be indentified as Author of this work has
been asserted by him/her in accordance with the Copyright,
Design and Patents Act 1988.

SAGE Publications Ltd
1 Oliver's Yard
55 City Road
London EC1Y 1SP

SAGE Publications Inc.
2455 Teller Road
Thousand Oaks, California 91320

SAGE Publications India Pvt Ltd
B 1/I 1 Mohan Cooperative Industrial Area
Mathura Road
New Delhi 110 044

SAGE Publications Asia-Pacific Pte Ltd
33 Pekin Street #02-01
Far East Square
Singapore 048763

www.luckyduck.co.uk

ACC. NO. 8121970X   FUND HDEC
LOC. ET   CATEGORY WEEK   PRICE £17.99

2 5 APR 2008

CLASS No. 372. 832 COL
OXFORD BROOKES
UNIVERSITY LIBRARY

British Library Cataloguing in Publication data

A catalogue record for this book is available from the British Library

ISBN 978-1-4129-4630-8

Library of Congress Control Number: 200794084

Commissioning Editor: George Robinson
Editorial team: Mel Maines
Illustrations by: Philippa Drakeford

Typeset by C&M Digitals (P) Ltd, Chennai, India
Printed in India at Replika Press Pvt. Ltd
Printed on paper from sustainable resources

Contents

Acknowledgements

Frances Hillier, without whom this book would not have been written; for her input and enthusiasm, her knowledge about the situation in Africa, the story of Pumela and the case study in the Appendix.

Martin Pitman, headteacher and Christian Malone, deputy of Milford on Sea C of E School, for their willingness to talk about their global citizenship and their help during visits.

Claire Painter, headteacher of Rowledge C of E School, Hants, for her help and enthusiasm and for sharing the many ideas in use at that school.

Janet Roberts, headteacher and Kath King of All Saints C of E Junior School, Fleet, Hants, for sharing all they do in their school under the heading of global citizenship.

The headteacher of Bulford C of E Primary School, Bulford, Wilts, for allowing me to visit and Janette Diomede, deputy head, for showing me around their school, sharing children's work together with a PowerPoint presentation of their link with a school in Africa.

Teacher reviewers for their ideas and suggestions.

George Robinson for helping to incorporate his own suggestions as well as ideas from teacher reviewers.

About the author

Margaret Collins was a headteacher in infant/first schools. She is now Senior Visiting Fellow in the School of Education at the University of Southampton. She researches children's perceptions of health education topics, writes and co-writes teaching materials for children, books and articles on personal, social, health and citizenship education (PSHCE).

Let's learn about global citizenship

Introduction

The report of the Advisory Group on Education for Citizenship and the Teaching of Democracy in Schools (see www.qca.org.uk/ages3-14/subjects/6123.html) identifies three inter-related components that should run through all education for citizenship:

- **Social and moral responsibility:**
  Pupils learning – from the very beginning – self-confidence and socially and morally responsible behaviour both in and beyond the classroom, towards those in authority and towards each other.
- **Community involvement:**
  Pupils learning about becoming helpfully involved in the life and concerns of their neighbourhood and communities, including learning through community involvement and service to the community.
- **Political literacy:**
  Pupils learning about the institutions, problems and practices of our democracy and how to make themselves effective in the life of the nation, locally, regionally and nationally through skills and values as well as knowledge – a concept wider than political knowledge alone.

Pupils develop skills of enquiry, communication, participation and responsible action through learning about them and becoming informed and interested citizens. This will be achieved through creating links between pupils' learning in the classroom and activities that take place across the school, in the community and the wider world.

Every Child Matters (DfES, 2003–2006) states that 'children and young people have told us that five outcomes are key to well-being in childhood and later life – being healthy; staying safe; enjoying and achieving; making a positive contribution; and achieving economic well-being.' Under 'Make a positive Contribution' in the Outcomes Framework of that document, five aims are highlighted:

- engage in decision making and support the community and environment
- engage in law-abiding and positive behaviour in and out of school
- develop positive relationships and choose not to bully or discriminate
- develop self-confidence and successfully deal with significant life changes
- challenges develop enterprising behaviour.

This book will go a long way towards helping teachers to achieve these aims with their young pupils.

Citizenship education is about helping young people to understand their rights and responsibilities, to understand how society works and to play an active role in society. Education about citizenship will help children to:

- recognise their worth as individuals, knowing that they are unique
- understand that we are all different in many ways
- see things from other people's point of view
- recognise right from wrong and to have the confidence to choose right
- understand that they have rights and responsibilities
- understand the democratic process
- recognise that we have a multicultural society where everyone is equal
- understand that we can all learn from other races and cultures
- help developing countries to realise their potential
- recognise that they will have a part to play in working towards world peace.

Citizenship education equips children and young people with the knowledge, understanding and skills to play an active part in society as informed and critical citizens who are socially and morally responsible. It aims to give them the confidence and conviction that they can act with others, have influence and make a difference in their communities.

From www.qca.org.uk/ca/subjects/citizenship

The UN Convention on the Rights of the Child states that:

All children and young people have the right to have a say in the decisions that affect them, to access relevant information and to express their feelings. This statement includes all the children in the world.

Lessons in citizenship will help children to become better informed, to take part in discussions as they express their views and listen to the views of others. They will recognise the choices they can make and the difference between good and bad choices and how these affect themselves and others. Children will come to understand they are a valued contributor in making their school community a welcoming, safe and fair learning place for all.

They will learn how their community is organised and what they can do now with the help of their families, or by themselves as they grow older, to influence how democracy works. They will learn about the different communities of home, school, neighbourhood, regional, national and international communities. They will begin to understand the importance of looking after the local and wider environment.

In our multicultural society it is even more important to include a citizenship strand in the PSHE (Personal, Social and Health Education) curriculum. Citizenship, with its emphasis on teaching social and moral values, is important, especially with the kinds of racial tension seen in the UK as well as the wider world. It is not sufficient to wait until students are in secondary school to educate them about citizenship; it should be started immediately and with the youngest children at an appropriate level as soon as they start school.

Circling around Citizenship[1] offered some citizenship activities for children aged four to eight but these did not contain any reference to global citizenship. This book starts with what the children already know and examines citizenship issues in the children's own situation before moving on to think about the wider world and the global implications.

Before starting this book I visited several primary schools where children were working towards a greater understanding of global citizenship. There were as many ideas as the schools I visited,

---

[1] Collins, M (2002) *Circling Around Citizenship*, Lucky Duck Publications, Bristol

could
have
done
this
-in
here

but one thing that was true in all circumstances is that they believed in making contact between the children in their school and either another school or country, to try to give the children a better understanding of what the 'global' in global citizenship is all about.

Some schools had made contact because their teachers had visited; one linked with a church or mission in another country; one linked with a school in the UK. Some small schools in one area formed a shared link. In some cases two or more teachers visited each others' schools in other countries, in others UK teachers visited the other country's school. Yet it seems to me that, for young children, it is not sufficient just to have a teacher contact but imperative to have a child link and preferably because each child has visited the other's school and neighbourhood.

It is by learning about lives in other communities, first hand, that the best kind of understanding can take place. In terms of global citizenship it is important to remember that children will need opportunities to understand and appreciate the socio-economic differences between groups of people and schools as well as learning to understand and appreciate the lives of people in various ethnic groups in our multicultural society.

If we agree that it is important to start where the children are, perhaps contact should be with a class in a school in a different part of their own area. Twinning country children with those from urban areas, for example, could provide understanding and acceptance of a different way of life. Young children could visit each others' school and get to know the mores of that school and neighbourhood. Respecting and accepting the differences between children in their own class would be a very good starting point for the youngest children.

In schools where there are various cultures, children should include, respect and learn about all the represented societies within their school environment. Schools in a multicultural society may have many and varied ethnic societies represented. We have much to learn from and about each other both within each school and also between nearby schools with a different catchment.

As the children grow, the link could be with a class in a school in a different town in the UK; one with a very different catchment area. Visits could be exchanged after introductory written contact possibly by email or fax. There would be great benefits to pupils and staff if some of the schools with high ethnic populations were to be twinned with schools with small numbers of, or no, ethnic pupils. Reciprocal day or longer visits would be beneficial.

Parents should also be involved wherever possible. Where parents find written or spoken English difficult, translators may need to be found. Notices and letters home may need to be in the children's first language. All parents have a lot to offer schools; parents of children from other cultures, with help, may be able to offer a great deal to the school in many ways.

Many villages and towns have twinned themselves with a town or village abroad; teachers could twin their class with a class in a school in that town or village. Physical links would be important even if there could only be one visit each way. To be twinned with a school with a common language would make life easier. Communication in English by email gives immediate contact; better than letters that take a long time to arrive.

The DfEE publication *Developing a global dimension in the school curriculum* contains advice on how to implement a global thrust to citizenship with several examples of what schools are already doing in schools of all age groups. Their eight Key Concepts are Citizenship, Sustainable Development, Social Justice, Diversity, Values and Perceptions, Interdependence, Conflict Resolution and Human Rights. Activities on all these issues are to be found in this book.

Fountain (1994) states that 'it is thought that children under seven, who learn through their senses via first hand experience of their immediate environment, cannot grasp abstract notions about justice, rights, resource distribution and interdependence. Or can they?'

She illustrates how they can by listing the daily concerns of young children which have parallels on the global level:

Nursery and infant children regularly:

- call each other names, sometimes gender or race related (prejudice)
- exclude others from play for arbitrary reasons (discrimination)
- argue over materials (resource distribution)
- protest that rules are 'not fair' (human rights)
- fight (peace and conflict)
- use consumable materials, sometimes unwisely (environmental awareness)
- find that by sharing and working together, more can be accomplished (interdependence)
- negotiate to find a solution to a problem that both parties will find acceptable (perspective consciousness)
- discover that some adults in school have power in the school to make decisions or that older children may be allowed to do things that younger ones are not ('state of planet' – or in this case 'state of school' – awareness)
- decide what activities they will take part in; write letters, pick up litter or plant flowers in the school grounds (awareness of human choice and action).

While most teachers understand that working on these issues is paramount, few draw on examples of children's own actions to help them to understand the global parallels.

Fountain goes on to say that three areas, self-esteem, communication skills and co-operation, stand out in particular as areas which can be developed in young children and 'prepare children to participate more effectively in the interactive learning strategies employed in the field of global education'.

This book tries to dwell more on celebrating and understanding children and people in the developing countries; they do not need our pity but they do need our understanding and our help to try to redress the balance between the 'haves' and the 'have-nots'. We must not protect children too much from the realities of the world. They see much in news items on the TV that needs to be explained to them. Do they only see the poverty of starving Africans or can they also be helped to understand the rich culture of these countries with their very different daily lives? Do they understand that children living in cities in developing countries have lives rather similar to their own?

National Healthy School Standard (NHSS)

The National Healthy School Standard website states that to meet the NHSS standard for PSHE and citizenship, the school must recognise that:

- 'all aspects of school life have an impact on the personal and social development of pupils and that consistent messages are presented
- all aspects of school life can have an impact on the development of pupils in becoming informed, active and responsible citizens'.

The school must show that they provide

- 'opportunities for pupils to be actively involved in the life of their school'.

The activities in this book will help teachers to meet these requirements.

4

The International School Award (ISA)

Supported and funded by the DfES since 1999, this scheme provides recognition for teachers and their schools working to instill a global dimension into the learning experience of children. By December 2005, awards had been granted to 670 successful schools. The school's international co-ordinator will find opportunities for professional development, including study visits while the whole school is supported as the international dimension is established. See www.globalgateway. org.uk/Default.aspxage=1343

Other useful websites include www.wiredforhealth.gov.uk and www.teachingcitizenship.org.uk.

Want to get really involved?

Born in what is today the Czech Republic, Johan Amos Comenius (1592–1670) was an educator who worked for peace and unity between nations. He was convinced that education was the only way to achieve full human potential. Visit the comenius website below to find out what opportunities are available within the countries in the EU.

Comenius 3 supports European networks of organisations involved in Comenius that share expertise and good practice.

For other kinds of involvement, visit these websites:

Voluntary Service Overseas, www.vso.org.uk/

Global Eye, http://www.globaleye.org.uk

LINK community development, www.lcd.org.uk/

http://www.britishcouncil.org/home/learning/socrates/ socrates-comenius.htm see also website: http://ec. europa. eu/education/programmes/llp/comenius/index_ en.html

The following are two extracts from the National Curriculum, PSHE, which are directly covered in this book.

KS1. Preparing to play an active role as citizens

Pupils should be taught:

- to take part in discussions with one other person and the whole class
- to take part in a simple debate about topical issues
- to recognise choices they can make and recognise the difference between right and wrong
- to agree and follow rules for their group and classroom and understand how rules help them
- to realise that people and other living things have needs, and that they have responsibilities to meet them
- that they belong to various groups and communities such as family and school
- what improves and harms their local, natural and built environments and about some of the ways people look after them
- to contribute to the life of the class and school
- to realise that money comes from different sources and can be used for different purposes.

KS2. Preparing to play an active role as citizens

- to research, discuss and debate topical issues, problems and events
- why and how rules and laws are made and enforced, why different rules are needed in different situations and how to take part in making and changing rules
- to realise the consequences of anti-social and aggressive behaviours, such as bullying and racism, on individuals and communities
- that there are different kinds of responsibilities, rights and duties at home, at school and in the community, and that these can sometimes conflict with each other
- to reflect on spiritual, moral, social and cultural issues, using imagination to understand other people's experience
- to resolve differences by looking at alternatives, making decisions and explaining choices
- what democracy is, and about the basic institutions that support it locally and nationally
- to recognise the range of national, regional, religious and ethnic identities in the United Kingdom
- that resources can be allocated in different ways and that these economic choices affect individuals, communities and the sustainability of the environment
- to explore how the media present information.

What you get in this book

This book explores, with activities, six aspects of global citizenship, namely:

- Basic needs
- Environmental issues
- Fairness
- Exploring various cultures
- Democracy
- Global issues.

Each section has an introductory page with the main focus and a list of the themes within it. Where relevant, there are suggestions of useful organisations and websites. These websites existed at the time of going to print; users should check website references to see if they have changed, substituting others if appropriate. There is also a further list of websites in the Appendix.

Each of the six sections is divided into topics with activities. It is hoped that the topics will prove to be a jumping-off point, stimulating teachers and encouraging children to go wider in their learning. Depending on the circumstances at the time and in the location of the school, teachers will be able to use these activities to set the children further challenges; to help them to explore the current situation and to help with understanding the concerns that are relevant at that time.

There is considerable overlap between the sections and although teachers might like to concentrate on one section, a glance at the others to find related activities could be useful.

Each section has activities, with those suitable for younger children, aged four to six, on the left-hand page. Those for older children aged seven to nine on the right-hand page include a home learning activity to enable parents and families to be involved. This two-page format enables a 'mix and match' approach, with teachers taking from both pages activities suitable for their particular children. (Many local authorities provide a translation service which could be beneficial here. Teachers could enlist the help of this service or use competent bilingual parents to write a translation of each home activity.)

The activities are also suitable for individual children with special needs to work through with a teaching assistant alongside to give help and discuss the meaning behind the activities.

In some cases, group or paired work is suggested. In these cases, teachers should organise flexible and various groups or pairs of children with differing abilities and backgrounds in each group. The children are asked to keep a list of those they work with. It is intended that every child will have worked with every member of the class by the end of the activities. This will help children to appreciate the concept of equality and inclusion. Ask children to design a simple sheet with columns to record this data. Alternatively you could choose one sheet to be duplicated for all children to use, with one sheet for names of all children they have worked with or duplicate a new sheet for each section.

At the end of each section there is a story for the children to consider with some follow-on activities. These stories can be used in various ways: you may like older children to write the story or a similar one in their own words, altering or suggesting a different ending and adding their own written comments. You could split each story into sections, asking groups of children to write and illustrate one part, making a cover and binding the whole to make a storybook for your class library. Younger children may be able to take a picture approach and draw a series of pictures to tell the story, perhaps each group drawing one picture to make a wall picture. You may like to put their drawings together to form a class picture reading book.

Each section has several activity sheets which are listed on the introduction page of each section. These activity sheets are an integral part of the activities and the text directs teachers to each sheet. In some cases they are more suitable for older or younger children and teachers of the other age group may like to use the activity sheet as a lesson idea, extension to their lesson or as a piece of work for children to take home to show their families.

At the end of each section a page of reflection activities asks children how they can get involved before suggesting a global challenge.

Children should make a Global Citizenship folder in which to put their work. If work is to be displayed or taken home it would be useful to make a photocopy for the folder so that a complete record of the global citizenship work is maintained.

More and more schools are using Circle Time as a venue for discussion which includes all the children. Citizenship/PSHE discussions can fit naturally into Circle Time with issues being discussed, further explored and extended during other lesson times. Many of the activities in this book can take place in Circle Time.

Circle Time is a structured, regular occasion when a class group meets in a circle to speak, listen, interact and share concerns. The circle is a symbol of unity and co-operation, indicating that the group is working together to support one another and to take equal responsibility for addressing issues; a very important aspect of citizenship. For help in understanding how to use Circle Time with young children, see *Circle Time for the Very Young*, 2nd edition and other books about Circle Time listed in the Appendix.

It is essential to have a world map and possibly a globe on display in the classroom. The children will need to refer to the countries and areas as they work through the activities so as large a map as possible is preferable.

Introductory activities

While you may prefer to choose activities from the various sections that are appropriate for the children you work with, it is important to set the scene with all children completing the two introductory activities.

If you have previously worked with the children on topics of similarities and differences, remind the children of this. There are many Circle Time games and activities that you can use to stress the superficial differences between children and people as well as making sure that we are all basically the same with the same needs, expectations, rights and responsibilities wherever we live and whatever race we originate from. Here are a few:

Change places

Stand up if you have blue eyes, change places with each other. Use other differing attributes.

Raise an elbow

Raise an elbow if you have ten toes, change places. Use other similar attributes.

Matching cards

Make a set of cards with pictures of people or faces cut from magazines for half the number of your children, cut each in half with a distinctive cut. Give out the cards and ask the children to quickly find their other half.

Finish the sentence

'I'm the same as everyone else because I ...'
'I'm different from everyone else because I ...'

Similarities
two eyes
two ears
a mouth
legs
feet
fingers
hair
teeth

Run around the circle

Stand up if you have, for example, long hair – run around the circle and back to your place.

Come to the middle

Come to the middle if you have a sister. Clap three times and return to the circle in a different place. Use other family members, pets, likes and dislikes.

Similarities and differences

Start in Circle Time.

Talk to the children about how they are the same and yet how they are all different and unique. Go around the circle asking the children to tell you one way in which they are all the same. Ask them to finish the sentence 'We are all the same ...' Make a list of what the children say. Now ask the children to think of one way in which they are different from someone else in the class. Ask them to finish the sentence.

'I am different from ... because ...'

Talk about all children, just like animals, being different, special and unique so that their parents can easily identify them. If you can find a copy of *No Two Zebras are the Same by Stig Andersson*[2], read it to the children. If not, tell the children that even zebras which look exactly the same to us are all different and unique.

Talk about people who come from different areas of the UK. Explain that the way they talk will differ slightly because of local accents. Can any volunteers give you examples of this? Explain that people from different areas may have different customs and ways of doing things. Can any volunteers give examples of this? Ask volunteers to tell you other ways in which people in this country can be different.

Ask and discuss these two questions:

'Are some people better than others just because they are different?'
'Are some people not as good as others because they are different?'

Talk about the importance of all human people being treated the same however different they may seem to be.

Explain the words 'citizen', 'citizenship' and 'global'. Say that you are going to be finding out about citizens in this and other countries and that this is called Global Citizenship. They will need to record the work they do in a folder.

---

[2] Andersson, Stig, (1980) *No Two Zebras are the Same*, Lion Publishing, Tring, UK

Making the Global Citizenship folder

First, select some books with artwork from different countries to display. Tell children that they will need some kind of folder for the work they do and that their first activity will be to make or decorate that folder. What title will they give their folder? Ask for suggestions and vote on which they think is the best.

Jenny McDonald
My Global
Citizenship folder

You may need to make these for very young children or give help to some children. The folder should be slightly larger than A4 with a pocket along each side into which papers can go.

Ask the children to decorate the front by drawing a picture of themselves in the centre and to add the title of the folder and to write their own name.

Explain that as this folder is for work about global citizenship and they might like to make a decorative border around their folder to show this.

Ask them to look at the books you have selected for them to help them to decide on which country's art work they will use for their design.

Older children can make the folder for themselves or you may prefer to use loose-leaf binders.

Ask younger children to draw a second picture to go inside their folder; a picture of themselves with their family. Help them to add labels showing how each person in the family is different.

Ask older children also to draw members of their family with a description of each of their physical characteristics.

Section 1

Basic needs

Focus

This section will help children to explore basic needs, what they are, whether wants are needs and how really basic needs are met or not met in various parts of the world:

Basic needs

- a home
- families, friendship and love
- healthcare
- clean water
- warmth and clothes
- education
- protection.

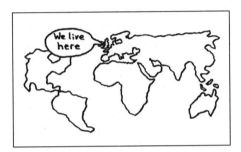

It is essential to have a world map on display in the classroom with each country clearly named. Help the children to realise where this country is on the map and where cold and hot countries are situated. Explain that some countries are rich countries where everyone has their basic needs satisfied but that some countries are very poor, where people are often cold and hungry, without shelter or enough food or clean water.

See the activity sheets at the end of Section 1, 'A home for me', 'I know', 'Education and learning', 'I can protect …'

Duplicate and cut out the 'Basic needs cards' on page 31 to use the reflection activity. http://www.globaldimension.org.uk/default.aspx?id=102 Visit this website to read about work on Rights and Responsibilities with Year 2 children.

Other useful websites:

http://www.centrepoint.org.uk/

http://www.homeless.org.uk/

http://www.homeless.org.au/runaways.htm

http://www.emmaus.org.uk/

N.B. Food is also a basic need but there are already many excellent resources in schools. You may like to discuss foods while working on basic needs.

Basic needs – younger children

A home

In Circle Time, ask the children to think about what people need to keep them well. Ask the children to finish the sentence:

'To keep us well, we need ...'

Make a list of what the children say. When children repeat what someone else has said, make a mark against this on your list. When everyone has had a turn, read through your list and talk about each item. Have they missed out anything? Have they included friendship or love? Are all the things on the list a 'basic need' or are some of them 'wants'?

Talk about the difference between needs and wants and ask if there are things they should take off the list.

Ask the children to think about their homes and what a house has to have to make it a home. Does it need: beautiful furniture, a place to cook, clean water, comfortable beds, a playroom?

> **To keep us well we need...**
> a home
> someone to look after us
> nice things to eat
> to keep warm
> clothes to wear
> somewhere to sleep
> somewhere to play
> toys
> holidays
> friends
> outings
> birthdays

Talk about the basic need of a home as a shelter, a safe place with clean water, somewhere to cook, to be sheltered and to sleep.

Ask the children to draw a home they would like to live in; you could use the activity sheet 'A home for me'. Share their drawings and ask if all the rooms are really necessary. Could one or two rooms do for everything? Ask them to put a green tick in all the rooms that are really necessary.

Ask the children to think about the different kinds of homes in this country; houses, bungalows, flats, mobile homes. Ask the children to think of holiday homes such as caravans, tents, chalets. Would they like to live in one of these holiday homes all the time, even in the winter? If so, why? If not, why not? What about people in other countries who have no proper house. What kinds of places are their homes? How will they feel about living there?

Ask the children to draw their home and write down which of the things they have in their home is a 'basic need'. Ask them to put this work in their folders.

Basic needs – older children

A home

Explain to the children that one of the basic needs of mankind is a home. Ask them to think of all the kinds of homes people have in this country and talk about these. You may like to use 'A home for me' activity sheet.

Now think about people in this country who are 'homeless'. What does 'homeless' mean? Can they think why some people have no homes? How can people help the homeless? What does the government do? What other organisations help people who are homeless?

People in other countries sometimes do not have homes as we know them. Talk about people who have no homes and how this has come about. Ask them to help you to make a list of why some people may have no home.

Read through the list and talk about how people who lose their homes must feel.

> **In other countries, homes are lost because of:**
> earthquakes
> natural disasters
> flooding
> tornados
> wars
> refugees leaving
> persecution

What do people do if their home is lost through some disaster? Who can help them? Do their governments help them? Are there charities that will help? Do people from other countries help?

Talk about people who live in very poor countries and who have no homes. What do these people do? Who can help them? Ask the children to find out about one country where people have no permanent homes. They can use the books you have provided, their local library and the Internet. Ask each child to think about how people with no home must feel. Ask them to write an illustrated story about someone who has no home and to put this in their folder.

Learning at home

Ask the children to find out about street children in other countries. They can use the Internet or books as well as asking parents and friends to help; give them the website addresses at the front of this section as a starter and ensure they understand how to do Internet searches. Help from an older member of the family would be desirable for the searches.

Basic needs – younger children

Families, friendship and love

Ask the children in Circle Time to think of their families. Ask them to think how many people are in their family including themselves and to raise a hand if there are two people, three people and so on in their family. Talk about this.

Explain that some families have a mother and father or step-parents but not all families have two parents. Not all families have parents who live with them. Some children have one parent or are orphans. Some children live with foster carers or in a children's home and these are their families. Ask them to close their eyes and think about their own family. Ask them to think about how they would feel if they didn't have someone to live with and to look after them. Ask them to finish the sentence:

'If I didn't have someone to look after me, I'd feel ...'

Remind them that there are many children in other countries who do not have families. Usually this is because their parents have died or are ill. Some children have older siblings or no one to look after them and have to try to find their own food and shelter. Explain that having a family or someone to look after us is a basic need but that there are children who do not have this.

Ask the children to draw their present family. Help them to write how they feel about having a family. Use the activity sheet, 'I know ...'

Tell the children that having friends is a basic need. Ask them to think of their friends and what they do together. Are they good to their friends? Ask them to finish the sentence:

'I am good to my friend because ...'

Ask the children to draw a picture of a friend and to write who this person is.

Explain that love is a basic need; we all need someone to love or care for us and someone to love in return. Explain that people with no families often stay together and help each other. In some countries children without families stay together and help each other to find food and shelter. Can your children tell you how they think children would feel if they had no family, just a friendship?

Ask the children to draw some of the people they love and to write their names. Tell them to put this picture in their folder after they have shown everyone.

Basic needs – older children

Families, friendship and love

Talk about the many different kinds of families there are. Some with two parents; some with one; some with step-parents; some with other children; some with no children; some with grandparents and other family members. Explain that your family is not only the people whom you live with, but the extended family of aunts, uncles and cousins. Talk about the supportive role of the family; how families stick together, help and care for each other. Use the activity sheet 'I know …'

Friends
family friends
children friends
neighbours
school friends
long time friends
new friends
friends in different groups
distant friends

Talk about some of the other countries of the world where death and destruction have separated families and caused many people to have no family at all. How do your class think children with no family would feel? Ask them to finish the sentence:

'I think they would feel …'

Ask the children to imagine being a child in another country with no family at all, where people are poor. Ask them to write a story about such a person.

Explain that most humans need companionship and that means love or friendship. Ask the children to tell you how love and friendship can be the same and how they can be different. Ask the children to work in pairs to try to make two lists; one a list of friendship words and the other a list of love words. Do some words appear on both lists?

Talk about the different kinds of friends they have and ask each pair to write down each kind of friend and try to group these friends into some kind of order. Talk about neighbours as friends living nearby who often help and care for us.

Learning at home

Ask the children to find a story about a child from a different country who had friends who helped them and to write the title, author of the book and a short description to share later with the rest of the class. Ask them to write their own story of a friendship between children from different countries.

Basic needs – younger children

Healthcare

In Circle Time, write the word 'health' on the board and ask volunteers to say what they think this means. Write down what they say and help them to understand that good health means that they feel well in their body and that they also feel well inside their head (mental health).

Ask them to think about the things they can do to try to keep their body healthy and to finish the sentence:

'To keep healthy, I can ...'

Make a list of their suggestions to read at the end, amending any if necessary.

Now talk about what happens in this country if they are not well and ask volunteers to finish this sentence:

'If I am not well, I can ...'

Have they mentioned people who help them, such as doctors, chemists and dentists? Have they mentioned hospitals and nurses? Have they mentioned medicines and rest?

Ask them to help you to make a list of:

- all the people who help them if they are unwell
- all the things these people will do to help them if they are unwell.

Explain that in this country we have something called the 'National Health Service' which means that everyone who is sick can get help and medicines or hospital care to help to make them better.

Tell the children that people in some other countries do not have a scheme like this and that people cannot just go to the doctor or hospital if they are ill. Sometimes this is because there are not any doctors or hospitals; sometimes it is because it costs a lot of money to see a doctor or buy medicines and people who are poor cannot afford this.

Ask the children to close their eyes and think about a time when they were not well and had to have help. Ask them to open their eyes and tell you how they would have felt if they had lived in a country where there was no help. Ask them to draw themselves at a time when they were not well and to write about how they were helped to be made better. Ask them to put this in their folder.

Basic needs – older children

Healthcare

Write on the board the words 'National Health Service (NHS)' and ask the children to tell you what they think this means. Use their suggestions to help to explain this complex system whereby everyone can visit a doctor or a hospital and gain professional health care when they are ill or have an accident, whether they are rich or poor. Explain that in this country we believe that everyone has the right to medical help whenever they need it.

Tell them about the situation in this country before the NHS; that people had to pay the doctor to come and see them and to pay for any medicines they needed to make them better.

Help the children to understand that there are many countries that do not have a National Health Service and that in these countries children can be very ill and get no help at all to make them better; sometimes they die.

Talk about what we can do to make sure that we look after our bodies so that we stay as healthy and well as we can. Ask the children to work in pairs and to make a list of what they do. Share these lists in Circle Time and make one full list of all the ways we can try to keep our bodies healthy and well. Ask them to write out the full list to put in their folder.

Keeping healthy
Eat fruit and vegetables
Eat meat, cheese and eggs
Drink plenty of water
Wash hands before eating
Have exercise
Get enough sleep
Play with friends
Wear the correct clothes and shoes
Don't take risks.

Learning at home

Ask the children to choose one country where they do not have a health service and to find out from their families, books and the Internet what people there may have to do when they or their children are sick. Ask them to write down why some of them become sick, ill or have an accident and what they can do in their country if this happens. Ask them to find out if people in developed countries ever help and to list the kinds of things that people in other countries could do.

Basic needs – younger children

Clean water

In Circle Time, ask the children to think about where water comes from. Ask volunteers to tell the class. Talk about each suggestion.

We use water for...
drinking
washing
cooking
washing clothes
swimming
playing
watering plants

Explain that rain and river water are collected in reservoirs, cleaned and purified and sent to the taps in houses in this country and that our water is pure enough to drink from the tap. Tell the children that not many countries have water that is so pure and ask them if they have visited other countries where people do not drink tap water. Where do they get drinking water? List the names of these countries.

Ask the children to finish the sentence:

'We use water for ...'

Make a list of their responses.

Ask the children to draw themselves doing something with water and to write a caption for their picture. Share these in Circle Time before the children put their pictures into their folder.

Ask children to work in pairs to think of a slogan to help people to be careful not to waste water. Help them to write their slogan down and pin these on a wallboard. As a class read all the slogans and decide which says it best. You may need to put words from more than one slogan to make a good one. Ask children to write this slogan on paper (or duplicate a copy for each child) and ask them to illustrate the class slogan and take home to show their families before putting in their folder. Display one copy for everyone to see.

Ask the children to think about what would happen if the rain didn't fall for a whole year and to finish the sentence:

'If rain didn't fall for a year ...'

Tell the children about countries where this happens and where people do not have any water at all and that the water they do have is often dirty and not fit to drink. Because of this the plants won't grow and there is little food. Do the children think it is fair for people to have to live without clean water? What could be done about this?

Basic needs – older children

Clean water

Visit www.southernwater.co.uk for educational resources and information. Start by reminding the children about this basic need; water for cooking and cleanliness and the importance of clean drinking water. Explain that all habitable countries have some rain but sometimes there is very little. Help them to understand that not only people need water. Crops and animals need water too. Some countries will have droughts and not only humans suffer.

Experiment by planting a few cress seeds in three pots. Ask the children to water one pot, to overwater one pot and to leave one pot unwatered. Keep a diary for two weeks about the growth of the seeds and discuss their growth.

Use a rain gauge to measure the rainfall in your area for half a term. Ask them to keep a daily record of this rainfall for their folders and at the end of the half term ask them to find the total rainfall. Do they think this is enough?

Ask the children to think about how many litres of water they use each day and to write this down. In a maths session ask them to work out how much water they use in a week, month, year; how much their family uses and how much the whole class, then the whole school, use in a year. Is there enough to waste?

Ask children to think of ways of conserving water in this country. Do they always turn the tap off? Do they keep it running while they clean their teeth? On average a person uses 160 litres of water a day (*source*: Southern Water).

Investigate rainfalls and talk about places where there is too little rainfall. What do people do in those countries? Ask them to use an atlas to find out and list the places that have too much water and too little water.

Learning at home

Ask the children to talk to parents and friends, use books and the Internet to find out which countries are short of water. They could visit websites such as http://wellsforindia.org/

Ask them to find out what happens to the crops and the people in these countries. Do other countries help? Ask each child to choose one country where there is not sufficient rainfall and to investigate what people do to get enough water to survive. Share this work, reminding the children that water is a basic need.

Basic needs – younger children

Warmth and clothes

Talk with the children in Circle Time about the differences between summer and winter.

Ask them to finish the sentences:

'In winter ....'

and

'In summer ...'

Then ask them to tell you the various ways we keep warm in winter. Make a list of these.

In summer we wear shorts and T shirts.

Ask them to think about people who live in other countries where it is very cold in winter, such as Norway and Iceland. How do these people keep warm?

Ask the children to think about the difference between summer and winter clothes. Go around the circle with the children finishing the sentences:

'In winter we wear ...'

and

'In summer we wear ...'

Ask them to make two pictures of themselves; one a picture of themselves dressed for winter and the other dressed for summer. Ask them to lay out these pictures on their tables so that everyone can go around and see them before they put them in their folders.

Explain that in some cold countries the people have developed special knitting to keep them warm in the winter weather. In other countries people make special warm clothes from wool and skins. In some of the poorer countries the people often do not have warm clothes and warm homes. Look at your world map and help the children to find these countries.

Explain that being warm is a basic need but that in some countries people do not have warm homes and warm clothes and can become ill when it is very cold, especially if they don't have much to eat.

Ask the children if they think it is fair for people to be cold in the winter because they do not have enough money to buy warm homes, to buy fuel to heat their homes and to have warm clothes. Can they think of what could be done about this?

Basic needs – older children

Warmth and clothes

Explain that most countries have modern cities where people live, as we do in this country, where all their basic needs are met, but that in some areas of the country, away from the cities, there are people who live without these things. Look at your world map and try to identify the countries where people do not have enough money to make sure they have a warm home and warm clothes.

Are they surprised that some of these countries get cold in the winter? Explain that many places can be hot in the daytime but at night, when the sun goes down, they can be very cold places.

Remind the children about the people who live in tents or shelters in some countries and ask them to imagine how it must feel when the sun goes down and the night is cold. Ask the children to give you words to describe how people who are very cold might feel; collect these to make a list. Ask them to use some of these words to write a poem about being cold. Some might like to write a haiku.[3]

Cold feelings
miserable
freezing
horrible
icy
chilly
bitter
nippy
frosty
cold
raw
frozen
ice cold

Poem in three lines
Five syllables, then seven
Five again. No rhyme

Night is cold and dark.
Winter is the time I hate.
Summer time is best.

Learning at home

Remind the children that people have the right to be warm with warm clothes in this country but that not all people are so fortunate. Explain that sometimes old or unwanted clothes and objects are given to organisations to either give to other people or to be sold to make money to give to people in need in this or other countries. Ask the children to find out about these organisations in your area and to make a list of them. Ask them to ask their families what they do with their unwanted clothes, toys, books, furniture and objects and whether they give them to help people who need them. What else could they do with things they don't want any more? Could some be recycled?

---

[3] Eric Finney, born 1929

Basic needs – younger children

Education

Tell the children that another basic need is that of education. Explain that in this country children have to go to school as soon as they are five years old so that they can learn all the things they need to know for when they are grown up. Children in other countries are not all so fortunate. Tell them this story ...

> Meera lives in Rajasthan which is in north-west India. Half of the people in that country live in rural areas and Meera lives with her mother, her older sister and her brother in a small village called Phalom. Meera is six years old and really wants to go to school but her mother won't let her go. She says she needs her at home to look after the baby and the animals and to get the water from the well. A few boys from their village do go to school but not as many girls. It is a long way to walk in the hot sun. Some foreign aid workers built a new school in Bhalu and are trying to get more children to go there but Meera's mother won't let her. Meera sometimes feels very sad because she would really like to learn to read and write. Not many grown-ups can read in their village.

Ask the children how they would feel if they were Meera and to finish the sentence:

> 'If I were Meera I would feel ...'

Ask them to think about how they would feel if their parents and carers couldn't read stories to them.

> Some boys in Meera's village go to the school. Their parents think it's good for boys to learn to read and write and do maths; some people think girls don't need to go to school because they will soon be married and have their own babies and they don't need education for that.

Give each child a postcard-sized piece of card and ask them to make a postcard that they could send to Meera about your school. Ask them to draw a picture of themselves at school on one side of the card and to write a message to Meera telling her about your school and what they like to do. Ask the children to keep these in the folders.

> Dear Meera
> I like coming to school. We have books and games and toys here. I can read quite well. I am sorry you can't go to school.
> Here is a picture of me.
> from Jacques
>
> to Meera
> Phalom
> Rajasthan
> India

Help children to learn about Muluken from Ethiopia in interactive pages at http://www.oxfam.org.uk/coolplanet/kidsweb/muluken/muluken.php

Basic needs – older children

Education

Read Meera's story on the previous page to the children. Explain to them that many years ago in this country it was felt that only boys were worth educating. A few girls of rich parents would have had a governess and very few went to universities or colleges. Nowadays everyone in this country has the right to education and all children from the age of five years must attend school unless they are educated at home. Discuss the notion that 'only boys are worth educating'.

Ask the children to work in small groups and use the Internet and phone books to investigate the provision of education in your area and find out the answers to these questions: How many infant schools are there? How many junior schools are there? How many secondary schools are there? What colleges or universities are there in your area? Who pays for this education? Who else do we learn from? Discuss as a class before using the activity sheet 'Education and learning'.

Ask the children to work in pairs to investigate your school and make a report of their findings to keep in their folders. Ask them to find out about the people in the school, including all children and adults, as well as the number of children in each class, governors, building and playground provision.

Ask them to consider the life of children who live in other countries who cannot for some reason go to school. Ask them to think of why this might be. What could happen to the countries where the children are not educated and grow up unable to read, write and use maths and science?

Ask children to work in groups and make a list of the reasons why young people should be educated.

Learning at home

Ask the children to ask families, use books and the Internet to find out about how free education in this country has grown over the last two centuries. Are there any special people who have helped this? Have there been any government changes that helped this? Discuss their findings in Circle Time.

Basic needs – younger children

Protection

Write the word 'protect' on the board and ask the children if they can tell you what it means; make a list of what they say. Ask each child to use this word in a sentence, for example, 'I protect my books against the rain' and 'I protect my little brother when we cross the road'.

Explain that one of the basic needs is that we are protected from things that will harm us. Sometimes these protections are things such as walls around a pond so that people won't fall in and sometimes they are people who care for and look after others. Talk with the children about protection from wind and weather when they are outside and from harm in the place where they live. Ask the children to think of all the things that protect us – at home, on the streets, in traffic and around the town. Make a list under the heading, 'Things that protect us'.

'protect'
means to ...
keep safe
look after
save from harm
shelter
care for
watch over

Ask them to think about who protects them in various situations – in their home, on the roads, at school, in hospital. Ask each child to say who protects them in one of these situations. Ask volunteers to tell the class about other people who protect us, such as the police, neighbours and crossing patrols. Ask them to draw a picture of someone protecting a child at home or outside.

Ask them what happens if there are no parents or neighbours to protect them. Explain that our government has something called 'social services' with special people whose job it is to take care of people if they need looking after.

Explain that this protection is another basic need. Remind the children about those who live in some other poor countries where the government does not provide anyone to look after people in need. They may have no one to protect them if they have nowhere to live, are sick or have no food. They have to rely on their neighbours to help but what happens if their neighbours cannot help?

Ask them to do the activity sheet, 'I can protect ...' to put in their folder.

Basic needs – older children

Protection

In Circle Time, talk about protection as a basic need and ask children to volunteer to tell the class how they protect others and how others protect them while they are children. Use the activity sheet 'I can protect ...'

Who in this country is responsible for protecting children? Ask them to talk about this in their small groups and to make a list to share as a class. Do they know what happens if a child's parents die and there is no one to care for them?

Talk with the children about children who may well have parents, but who still need help. What do they do? Where do they go? They will probably know about Kidscape who help children with problems such as bullying. Do they know any more?

Discuss the problems of grown-ups who need protection. Perhaps they have no family, no home, no work and need help and protection. Ask children to find out about Social Services and how they can help people in need. There are other organisations who help people; in this country there is always some way of finding help and protection.

Remind them that children in other countries are not so fortunate and often have to fend for themselves at a very early age. They are often exploited and have to work for very little money, just to survive. Ask the children to think about how such a child would feel or how they would feel if they were that child. Ask them to write a poem or piece of prose about these feelings.

Learning at home

Ask the children to use all resources to find out about organisations such as Barnardo's, Kidscape and how our government provides specially trained people to help those who are ill, have a health condition or who have no home or money. Ask them to check with parents before putting 'street children' into a search engine. See http://street-children.org.uk/colombia.htm

Pumela's story

Read this story to the children and then carry out the activities below.

It is half past five in the morning and the sun is just about to come up over the huge, olive-green hills behind a small village called Engani, far out in the empty spaces of South Africa. Seven-year-old Pumela is already up and she quietly opens the thin wooden door that faces the sunrise. She can remember her father building the house and talking to her and her brother about the best place to put the door. 'When the sun wakes up, it is time to get up', he said, 'and that will be the first thing you see when you open the door. You must give thanks for each new day.'

Sometimes Pumela doesn't feel like giving thanks for a new day. Each day is so busy and she often feels very tired and hungry. Her first job is to go and get the water for the family. There is no water pipe in the village, so she dresses quickly, picks up the metal bucket and walks down the steep, narrow path to the river. She shivers; her dress is not really warm enough for these cold mornings. She hopes her father will send more money soon so that her mother can buy them all some warmer clothes. She pushes the bucket under the surface of the cold, murky water, waits until it is full then slowly and carefully lifts it on to her head. It is very heavy but she has been doing this for more than two years and already has a strong neck. She walks slowly back up the dusty slope to her home. She cannot move her head but she knows that the small, round, bright white house at the top of the hill is where she is heading for.

Pumela loves the smooth, round shape of the wall that protects them all. In the hot season it is cool in the one round room and now, in the winter, it shelters them from the cold of the early morning and the freezing nights. She was too young then to help make the bricks and plaster for the wall, but her ten-year-old brother, Sipho, often boasts of how he helped to build the house and pass the long bundles of grass up to his father to thatch the roof. It is a quiet and lonely place, there are hardly any roads and few visitors come here.

School starts at 7.45 and before that she has to make the mealie meal porridge for her two little brothers before ironing her school uniform and her brother Sipho's with the heavy metal iron that she warms over the fire. Ironing doesn't take long because all washing is laid out on warm stones in the sun beside the river to dry and so is not very creased. Sipho makes the two little ones get washed and dressed and rolls up their grass sleeping mats. Her mother will leave them at their grandmother's house on her way to her job picking potatoes at the big farm three km away.

Their father works away in Cape Town. Sipho wants to go and visit him and see the factory where he makes metal souvenirs for the tourists. Father is so busy working that he can't visit them often but sometimes he sends money for their food and clothes. Pumela offers to go to the Post Office after school to see if there is a brown envelope for them. The key to their post office box hangs on a grass necklace and she is now trusted to wear it tucked inside her school shirt. Last year she had learnt her numbers from 100 onwards and can now reach high enough to unlock box 107 which belongs to their family.

Soon Sipho and Pumela are ready to go to school. It is an eight km walk to the primary school. It is August which means it is still winter and the temperature is freezing as they set off. They know they will have to remove their fleece hats and gloves when they get there. They both have small pieces of rag in their blazer pockets, to clean the dust off their shiny black shoes when they get to school. They carry plastic bags containing their homework exercise books, a tiny stump of pencil and a ruler.

As they get near to their school, they can see its name, picked out in white chalk stones on the hillside. They start to run as they can see other children beginning to line up for assembly on the dry, brown-gold grass in front of the school. They know that if they are late they may not be let in. They slide into their class lines just in time and a single voice starts the first line of the hymn. The sound grows and grows and soon the bright blue sky is alive with the voices of 500 young children singing the Lord's Prayer. It is already beginning to get warmer outside in the fields.

After the prayers, reading and notices, they file silently into the cold, dark classrooms. These have no doors or glass windows; just an open doorway and windows with honeycombed breeze blocks to let in some light and allow air to circulate. It is dark and very cold until the sun gets higher. Pumela is lucky as they have enough desks and benches for her class if they squash up close. Sipho is in the oldest classroom where some of the children have to sit on the earth floor.

Pumela likes reading but is sad because there is only one textbook for each class. The teacher uses that to copy exercises onto the old, scratched, green board with smudgy chalk but it is sometimes difficult to read the words from the back of the class.

She has never had a book all to herself and hopes that one day she will pass all her exams to go to the Senior School where she's been told they have more books. In her class there are 75 children. She is one of the youngest but there are also some older boys who are over 15. They have still not passed their exams but as there are no jobs for them in the village they prefer to come and sit with their younger friends in the classroom.

At break time the teacher usually takes them outside to sit on the grass under the tree in the field. Pumela and Sipho begin to warm up and watch as the youngest children are given a slice of bread and some milk. Back inside the school they, and many of the other older children, find it hard to concentrate towards midday as they are so hungry. There are still two hours to go before they can go home to have a slice of bread with their grandmother.

Activities

Ask all the children to think about the difference between their school and Pumela's school. List and discuss these differences.

Ask younger children to draw a picture of Pumela's school and help them to write a sentence about it. Ask older children to write about the differences between Pumela's day at school and their own.

Talk about the rights of children to go to school and get an education. Remind them of the story of Meera and how children in some countries have to work for their parents even when they are very young. They cannot go to school.

You could ask children to vote on the best pieces of work to use to make a class book for the book corner or ask children to put it in their folder.

Basic needs – Reflection

Before Circle Time ask the children to look through their folders and read what they have written and to begin a list of all the children they have worked with in this section. In Circle Time have a general discussion about all the issues in this section. Ask the children how they feel about living in this country with all their basic needs met. Ask them how they would feel if they lived in a different place where none or only a few of these needs were met.

Ask the children to write a poem, song or a piece of prose that describes their feelings about living in a country where people are cared for.

Ask the children to work in small groups and make a list of all the basic needs they have learned about. Can they add others? As a class, amalgamate the lists. Display this in the classroom; ask children to copy it to put in their folder.

Duplicate and cut out the 'basic needs' cards and give each group a set of cards. Ask each group to put the cards in an order of their choice and to say why they have chosen this order. Discuss their ordered lists.

Use the cards to make a group game for five to eight people. The group sits in a circle either on the floor or around a table. Place the pile of cards face downwards in the centre. The first person takes the top card and reads it out. The second person tells the group how we in this country make sure that this need is met. The next person tells the group what can happen if it is not met. The third person tells the group who makes sure that this basic need is met. The fourth person takes the next card and so on.

Getting involved – global challenges

Ask the children if they can think of any ways that we could help other countries to ensure that basic needs are met. Does our government help? What kinds of things could they do when they grow up to try to make sure that people in all countries have their basic needs met? Is there anything that they can do now in any of the areas they have worked on in this section?

You might like to check out some websites, for example http://www.oaza.com/about.html.

Basic needs cards.
Duplicate on card and cut out.

nutritious food	clean water	clothing
warmth	safety	love and care
health care	security	family
education	medicines	cultural life
rest	a home	play

A home for me

Draw the kind of home you would like to live in. Draw all the rooms, the furniture and any outside things you would like. Make a list of these. On the other side, draw the smallest home that you can think about with just the things that are really needed.

Things I would like are ...

I know ...

Draw a friend or someone in your family and write what you know about them.

Do some more on the other side.

This is a picture of	I know
This is a picture of	I know
This is a picture of	I know

Education and learning

How do you learn? Who helps you to learn? Write in these boxes.

From my family I learn ....

From my teachers I learn ....

EDUCATION

From my friends I learn ....

From ....I learn .....

I can protect ....
Draw someone protecting you. Write what they are doing.

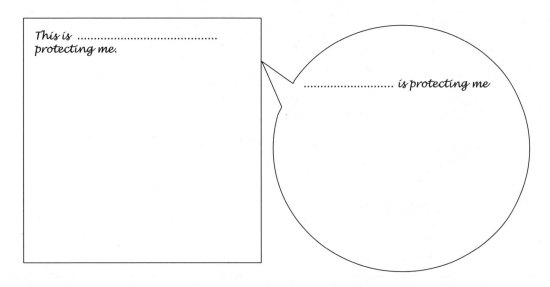

This is ....
protecting me.

.... is protecting me

Draw yourself protecting someone or something. Write what they are doing.

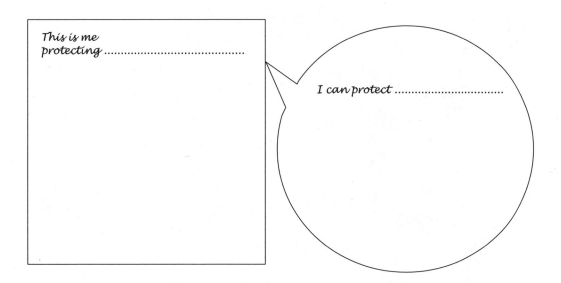

This is me
protecting ....

I can protect ....

Turn over the paper and draw a picture of you protecting yourself. Write what you are doing to protect yourself.

Section 2

Environmental issues

Focus

This section will help children to think about the environment and recognise the part they can play in caring for and protecting our world.

In this section the children first look at what the environment is before going on to explore the various kinds of environments and how these need protecting, under the headings:

- local environment: school, home, community
- worldwide environment
- ecology – local and global
- preservation of species
- water – sanitation, fun
- recycling – re-use; recycle; donate
- litter and rubbish
- food miles.

> Why not appoint an 'ecomonitor' in each class for a week's eco duties? The ecomonitor, wearing a badge or special hat, can be responsible for making sure lights are turned off, water taps are turned off and litter is not left about.

See the activity sheets, 'Do you use water wisely?' and 'Litter grid' at the end of this section.

This wonderful world

Environmental issues – younger children

Local environment

In Circle Time, write the words 'The environment' on the board and ask the children to tell you what they think this word means.

Make a list of what they say and talk about whether the children are correct, almost correct or not correct at all in what they offer. Explain that this word really means all around us, the places where we go, our homes, the countryside and towns.

Ask the children to think about the classroom environment and who looks after it to make sure that it is pleasant and a place where people want to be. Ask them to finish this sentence:

> 'One person who looks after our classroom environment is ...'

Have they included themselves?

Ask them to think of the part they can play in keeping the classroom environment a clean and happy place to be and talk about the kinds of things they do.

The environment all around us where we are our setting the classroom the park places we play our gardens outside

Ask the children to think about their home environment. Who keeps this place clean, tidy and beautiful? Is it the job of the grown-ups or do they have a part to play? What kinds of things can they do?

Move on to the environment outside the school; the area where they live, the streets, shopping parades and public areas. Who keeps these places clean, tidy and beautiful? What do these people do? Have the children a part to play in keeping the outside environment clean and tidy and beautiful?

Make two folds in pieces of A4 paper, making three sections. Ask the children to draw three pictures for three environments, their classroom, outside their school and their home. Ask the children to draw a picture in each section showing themselves doing something to improve the environment there. Help them to write a title, caption or speech bubble to show what they are doing.

Environmental issues – older children

Local environment

Ensure that all children understand what the word 'environment' means, if necessary do the first activity for younger children on the facing page.

Ask the children to work in pairs and to make a list of all the local environments they know. Ask each pair to share their list with another pair, crossing off all duplicates to make a new list. Ask each four to share with another four and do the same. Come together as a class and make one list of all the local environments.

Ask the children to work in their same pairs, choose one of the environments from their list, write and illustrate about who keeps this place safe, clean and attractive and what part they can play in this. You could use this work to make a wall picture of their work, first duplicating each piece of work to put a copy in each child's folder.

Ask the children to discuss who keeps the streets, drains and common areas clean and who organises for this work to be done. Who cuts and tidies trees and clears up fallen leaves? Who pays for all this?

Local environments
shopping centre
library
cinema
park
recreation centre
swimming pool
supermarket
High Street

Learning at home

Ask the children to look about them when they go home and to make a list of all the street furniture they see on their way, for example, bus shelters, lamp posts. Ask them to draw some of these from memory when they get home and to find out who provides and maintains these pieces of street furniture.

Back at school ask the children to share their homework and make a comprehensive list of all the street furniture they have mentioned. Discuss where the money comes from to provide and maintain these pieces of street furniture. Discuss what this country does to protect its environment and keep it a pleasant place. Talk about other countries that may do things differently. Do some countries have more money for their environment than others? Could something be done to make this fairer?

Environmental issues – younger children

Worldwide environment

Assemble a collection of books about different countries for children to refer to. In Circle Time, ask the children to think about the whole world as one big environment. On the world map, find and name this country and other countries. Ask children where they and their families were born and where they have visited; use pins and coloured threads to link family birth places and visited places to the children's names. Ask children to tell the circle what they know about these countries.

Explain that the UK is neither cold nor hot; it has a temperate climate. Ask the children to use the map to help you to make a list of hot countries and a list of cold countries. Ask the children to think about how people live in cold countries in the winter.

What is it like? What do they do? Collect responses.

Talk about going to school in the dark and having to wear lots of clothes and explain that in schools in these cold countries, the children usually leave all their warm outdoor clothes in special warm rooms to dry while they are inside; they have to put all these clothes on again every time they go outside. In Norway, in some schools older nursery and infant children go outside for two or more whole days each week to do creative play activities in the woods, even when it rains or snows.

Talk about summertime in northern countries such as Norway, Sweden and Iceland. Do they know that flowers and plants lie sleeping under the winter snow and only begin to grow again when the snow has melted and the short summer brings new buds, flowers, seeds and fruits? What about birds?

Winter in cold countries
ice
snow
long, dark nights
short days
not much sun
wear lots of warm clothes
cars with chains
snowploughs
snowmen
icicles
ski-ing
ice skating
sledging

Ask the children to do the above activity with summer in cold countries before looking at how people live in summer and winter in hot countries. Working in fours, ask children to make a set of pictures of winter or summer in a hot or cold country, each child doing one. Assemble each set of pictures to talk about.

Environmental issues – older children

Worldwide environment

Ask the children to do the first activity from the previous page and to link their birth places to their name on the world map. Talk about the northern hemisphere and ask the children to tell you what they know about people's lives in these countries. Do the same with the southern hemisphere.

Explain that some of the countries are well developed and ask the children to help you to name these. Discuss the lives of the people in these developed countries. The UK is considered to be a developed country; ask the children to give their views as to why this is. What natural resources have helped the UK to develop? What kinds of things have the governments done to help this? Can the children name other developed countries and say why this is?

Some countries are still developing and their people may not have the advantages of a well-structured system; some are poor countries, others have rich, city areas and poor, country areas. Can the children name some of these countries?

Discuss how the lives of people in developed and developing countries are different and what causes these differences. One cause for differences is the natural resources of each country. Some underdeveloped countries are rich in natural resources yet poor in distribution of this wealth; others are poor in natural resources and their governments have not helped people to use what they have wisely; some have exploited them. People in some countries have seized the wealth of the country for themselves and their families, leaving other citizens poor. How could this be made fairer?

Learning at home

Ask each child to identify and name one developed country and one developing country. Ask them to use their families, books and the Internet to help them to find out and write about the contrast between the lives of the people living in each chosen country. Is the contrast always to do with the environment? You may like to help children to choose their countries so that as many as possible can be investigated in this way. Discuss their findings and use their data to make a wall display.

Environmental issues – younger children

Ecology – local and global

Explain to the children in simple terms what ecology is. Here we are finding out about how all things that grow, (people, animals and plants) relate to each other and their surroundings; how we and they depend on each other for survival.

Explain that many plants depend on insects for pollination so that fruits will grow. Tell them that the bees and butterflies they see in the garden are doing good work for gardeners as they transfer pollen, the 'magic dust', from plant to plant and help the plants' seeds and fruits to develop. Ask the children to think about what could happen if all the flying insects died out and to finish the sentence:

'If there were no insects ...' (e.g. there would be no apples)

Explain that birds make their nests in the springtime when there are plenty of insects, such as greenfly and caterpillars, around to be food for their nestlings.

Ecology is the scientific study of the distribution and abundance of living organisms and how these properties are affected by interactions between the organisms and their environment.

Talk about how different countries grow different plants because of the kind of weather and soil there is. Why won't oranges and bananas grow in this country? Why do great redwood trees grow in America? Why do people in some countries eat a lot of rice? Ask the children to draw pictures of three plants and three animals that live in this country and to write their names. Ask them to find out about and draw two plants, and two animals that live in other countries, to write their names and the country where they grow or live.

Make a game. Use small cards and ask the children to write the name of a country on one half; on the other half ask them to draw a picture of something from that country. Share their work, then cut each card in half with a distinctive cut so that it can be put together again. Use the cards for matching or as a group game, giving out all the pictures and asking children to find the country.

Explain about endangered species, such as the snow leopard, and help children to understand that all people in the world have a responsibility to make sure that all plants and animals are kept safe so that they do not die out.

Environmental issues – older children

Ecology – local and global

Explain that we are learning about how various living creatures and plants in our world depend on each other for survival. Read and discuss the definition on the facing page. Can the children give examples of how plants and animals depend on each other? For example, birds of prey take eggs and small animals as food for their young; dormice nest in farm crops to take advantage of the cover, house martins make their nests in farm buildings.

Ask the children to investigate the plants and trees in your school grounds. Ask them to draw, name and write about some of these. Widen the above activity by talking about five different kinds of growing things in this country: plants, trees, insects, birds and animals. Write down these five groups as headings and ask the children to sign up to one of the groups to find out as much as they can about this category of life in this country. Encourage them to use books and the internet as their sources of data. Ask each group to collect, discuss among themselves and present their data in an appropriate way. Ask each group to lay out their data, writing, illustrations and photographs to make a presentation to the class. Discuss ways in which members of each group may depend on another group for their survival. You may like to make a display of each area of their findings.

Expand the previous activity by asking the children to work in groups of eight or nine to find out about the wildlife and plants in a country of their choice. Help each group to write a plan of action or organisation so that they utilise their time well and don't duplicate each other's work; encourage them to subdivide into smaller groups or pairs. Display and discuss each group's findings.

Remind the children about food chains and how these can be disrupted when man uses chemicals to make our crops grow bigger or better. Is this a good thing for all the creatures who share the habitat? What could happen?

Learning at home

In school, list various environments in this country; a river, seaside, countryside, woodland, town, village or a country they know about. Ask each child to investigate how the living things in one area interact with each other.

Environmental issues – younger children

Preservation of species

In Circle Time, talk about how some plants and animals are becoming fewer and fewer. Ask the children if any of them can say why they think this might be.

Explain what the word 'extinct' means and remind the children about dinosaurs which became extinct millions of years ago because, we think, the climate and conditions where they lived changed.

Talk about the dodo which is now extinct. Tell them that a dodo was a large bird that couldn't fly which laid a single egg in a grass nest on the ground. It used to live in forests in Mauritius and waded in ponds to catch fish for its food. When Europeans landed in Mauritius in 1598 they hunted it for food. Animals from their ships ate the bird's eggs and eventually, by 1681 all the birds had been killed and there were no more eggs to hatch. A few years ago some bones of the bird were found and scientists are investigating this extinct species. The word dodo means 'fool' in Portuguese and it was perhaps called this because even though it was a very large bird, it couldn't fly and didn't run away from hungry hunters who caught it for food.

Talk to the children about other animals that are facing extinction, such as some of the large apes and the snow leopard and explain that there are many reasons for this. Sometimes it is because the habitat is spoiled, such as when forests are cut down or the wrong plants grown in an area where the species lived. Sometimes it is because other animals move in and take over, as when the grey squirrel became strong and took the food of the red squirrel. Sometimes it is because hunters kill the species for its skin, tusks or feathers.

Ask the children to draw a picture of a dodo and help them to write a little about it. Ask them to think about what mankind should do to save animals and plants from extinction. They themselves can't do much now because they are young but what kinds of things could other people do and what could they do when they are grown up?

Environmental issues – older children

Preservation of species

Discuss the extinction of some species of animals, plants and birds. *The Guardian*, March 16, 2006, stated that findings from a large study of butterflies showed seven out of ten UK species are in decline. They say that intensive farming, habitat loss and climate are to blame.

Ask the children to find out about the dodo from books, encyclopedias and the Internet and to write and draw about the species. This website is a good starter: http://www.pbs.org/wgbh/evolution/extinction/index.html.

Discuss the extinction of dinosaurs, probably as a result of climate or habitat change; ask them to consider what, if anything, we can learn from this.

Ask the children to work in small groups to find out what other species of animals, fish or birds are in danger of extinction and make a list of these, for example, tigers, elephants, snow leopards, polar bears, giant pandas, tuna, cod, whales. Ask pairs of children to choose one species from their list and to find out as much as possible about it, for example, where it lives, what it eats, how it is becoming endangered and how many are left. Ask them to arrange their data with illustrations to make an eye-catching display.

Talk with the children about what humans can do to stop the disappearance of species. Is this feasible? Can we make it happen? Is there anything they, as children, can do to help? Add any ideas to the display. Can you arrange for the children's work to be displayed in a local library or public place?

Ask the children to choose one species, by voting, and organise a campaign to try to stop the eradication of that species.

Learning at home

Ask children to enlist the help of families to find a way to help to preserve or protect this species. Perhaps they can 'adopt' an animal in a zoo, or publicise the danger to this animal. Ask them to make a poster or handouts. Ask them to think about what they can do when they are grown up to save this creature.

Environmental issues – younger children

Water – sanitation and fun
(visit www.southernwater.co.uk)

In Circle Time, remind the children of the work they have already done about clean water and explain that they will be thinking about other uses of water. Talk about hygiene, the need to keep ourselves clean and how we use water for that. Ask them to finish the sentence:

'We use water to keep clean when we ...'

Ask the children to draw a picture and write about one way of using water to keep clean.

Talk about how we now use water in the lavatories, to flush away our waste products. Explain that years ago we had no 'loos' and that people used to dig holes in the earth to bury their waste. Ask if they have ever been camping and had to do this. Ask if they have used special camping 'loos' where chemicals are used.

Talk about the ways we use water for fun. Can the children give examples of these by finishing the sentence:

'We have fun with water when we ...'

Collect their ideas to make a list; when everyone has had a turn read out the list and talk about each item.

'*We use water to keep clean when we ...*'
wash our hands
have a bath
take a shower
wash clothes
wash the floor
clean the car

Ask the children to choose one fun way of using water, to draw a picture of them doing this activity and help them to write a sentence about it. Share these pictures in Circle Time.

Ask the children to think about whether we waste water when we do these fun activities. Are we careful to control the amount of water we use or do we throw it away? Ask them to make a list of the fun things that we do that waste water, such as playing in paddling pools in gardens, having water fights. Ask them to make a second list of fun things we do that don't waste water, such as playing in the sea, fishing and boating. Talk about children in developing countries who do not have clean water on tap, have to carry all their water from a long way away and can never use water for fun. How would they feel about that?

Environmental issues – older children

Water – sanitation and fun

Remind the children of work they have already done about water and explain that now we are looking at how we use water for hygiene, sanitation and fun. Ask the children to find out what the words 'hygiene' and 'sanitation' mean. They mean almost the same.

Talk about how most people in this country have bathrooms and lavatories. Remind the children that this was not always so and that people many years ago had to wash in a bowl or tin bath; that lavatories were often at the bottom of the garden or across a yard and that sometimes these were shared.

> We think that 'hygiene' means keeping things clean.
> We think 'sanitation' means pure, sterile disinfected, without germs.

Remind them that some people in developing countries may not have access to water and may not have flushable 'loos' as we do in the UK. Ask them to close their eyes and think how they would feel if they were in one of these countries and they did not have water for sanitation. Talk about the reasons for this, for example, lack of rain may mean that all water is needed for drinking and cooking; distance from cities may cause poor infrastructure; money may not be available to develop better sanitation. Discuss what can happen where there is poor sanitation.

Talk about using water for fun and leisure. Ask the children, in small groups, to list how we do this in developed countries and to consider which activities actually waste water. Discuss their lists in Circle Time. Talk about developing countries where there is no clean water for fun – only water in rivers which may be polluted. Ask them to consider why some people do not have enough water for sanitation and fun. Ask them to write how they feel about this and to answer the questions: 'Is this fair?' 'How can things be changed?'

Learning at home

Ask the children to complete the water usage chart with help from their families. With climate change we may have less rain in future. How can they and their families use less water? Discuss this.

Environmental issues – younger children

Recycling – re-use; recycle; donate

In Circle Time, talk to the children about what they do with their unwanted toys. Go around the circle asking each child. (Allow them to 'pass'.)

I give my old toys to my brother.

Now ask them to tell you about the things that their families no longer want. What do they do with them?

Jot down a list of what the children say and when they've all had a chance to speak, go through the list and talk about each one.

- Ask the children to think about what can be done with their old woollen jumpers. Do they know that these can be collected, wool shredded and made into new yarn for knitting, making new clothes or carpets?

- Ask them to think about what can be done with old cans. Do they know that these can be recycled? Do you collect them in your school?

- Ask them to think about charity shops. Do they know that people give their unwanted goods to be sold and the money sent to developing countries?

- Ask them to think about kitchen waste. Do they know that this can be composted and that it will turn into good soil that will grow new plants?

- Explain about patchwork quilts and rag rugs made from scraps of old fabric.

Ask each child to draw themselves doing some recycling or re-using something of their own. Help them to write about what they have drawn, what they are doing, and how they will now use the thing they are recycling or re-using.

Make a big display using all the children's pictures. Write questions around the display so that other people will think about recycling.

Environmental issues – older children

Recycling – re-use; recycle; donate

Use any appropriate activities on the facing page to set the scene. You may like to visit http://www.recyclenow.com/

Talk about re-using things that are no longer useful in their present state, for example, using old shirts for dusters or for cleaning the car, re-using pretty buttons off old clothes, or pieces of curtain fabric for cushions. Ask the children if they can think of any ways that they or their families re-use things.

Can any children tell you about some furniture or article from their house that has been given a different use, such as an old chest being used in the garage? Make a list of what they say. Do they know that old railway sleepers can be used in the garden – can they think of anything else in the garden that is re-used, for example pots, water butts?

- Ask the children to think of something they have recycled during the last week or two. Ask volunteers to tell the group and say what they think happened to it.

- Ask the children if they have ever been to a council waste recycling depot. If so, ask them to say what they saw there and what happens to the things that people take there.

- Ask the children to design and make a poster urging people to re-use, recycle or donate and to take their poster home to share with their families.

- Ask them to think about people in developing countries where there are so few goods that everything possible is re-used or recycled. How do they feel about living in a developed country where we waste so much?

Learning at home

Ask the children to make something from recycled goods; perhaps patchwork or a toy made from wire, wood or junk and to bring this to school to show. Ask them to find out about how people in any developing country recycle goods.

Environmental issues – younger children

Litter and rubbish

In Circle Time, ask the children if they have seen any litter this morning. Ask volunteers to say what the litter was and where it was. What will happen to it if no one picks it up?

I saw a plastic bag on the pavement.

Talk about the time it takes for plastic to decay and that if this is left about it will stay there for the whole of their lives unless someone picks it up. Ask them if they would like to pick up other people's litter. Remind them that if they do this they should wear gloves and be careful that there is nothing dangerous in it. Tell them why they should wash their hands afterwards. Talk them through the litter grid at the end of this section.

What do they think of people who drop litter? What do they think these people should do? Ask the children to draw a picture of someone dropping some litter and to draw a grown-up telling them what to do with it instead of dropping it.

Explain the problem to wildlife of plastic bags, broken glass and other litter being dropped in the countryside. Ask them to think about what could happen to animals that try to eat plastic bags or step on broken glass.

Ask them to think about plastic bags. Do they know that we use 150 million of these each week in this country? Write this number for them. Then write 500 and tell them that this is the number of years it takes each bag to decay. Talk about taking plastic bags back to supermarkets to re-use. Do they know any schemes that tempt people to do this?

Talk about the rubbish collections in your area; is it every week or fortnight? Do people collect garden waste? What happens to bottles and glass? Does the council collect other kinds of waste? Ask them to think about what the council does with things that cannot be recycled or re-used. Do they know that this is all collected and put into great holes in the ground and covered over? What do they think about this?

Environmental issues – older children

Litter and rubbish

First discuss any appropriate activities on the facing page. Ask the children to write a definition of 'litter', what litter includes and to circle litter that can be recycled.

Discuss how dropping litter spoils the environment and can hurt wildlife.

Go on a litter walk. Wearing plastic gloves and with sacks, ask the children to accompany you around the environment near your school to identify and collect litter. Back at school, put the litter into categories, such as building materials, glass, cardboard, metal, paper, plastics, polystyrenes, pottery, rubber, wood. Note the number of items in each category. Could you interest a local newspaper in this project for the publicity?

Find out how long litter items take to degrade and present the results graphically. Make copies of the litter grid at the end of this section and ask children to work in pairs to discuss and complete it. Discuss as a class.

If your school is in a coastal area, visit the following website to find out about marine litter.

http://www.savethenorthsea.com/sa/node.asp?node=1389

*By litter we mean
paper
broken bottles
old cans
refuse
plastic bags
packaging
odds and ends
untidiness.*

Ask them to think about packaging that comes with foods. Is it all necessary? What happens to it? Can it all be recycled? Discuss your local council rubbish collections. Do people sort rubbish into types for disposal? How is this done?

Learning at home

Ask the children to find out if there are any partnerships with local providers in your area to deal with the collection and recycling of unwanted articles and rubbish and to write about these people and what they do. How many types of rubbish are collected and how? What kinds of bins, bags or boxes are used, where is this taken and how is it recycled? The rest of the rubbish that cannot be recycled doesn't just disappear! Ask them to write about what happens to it.

Environmental issues – younger children

Food miles

In Circle Time, ask the children if they can think what 'food miles' might be. Consider their responses; help them to understand that they are the miles that food travels 'from field to plate'. Explain that food which travels a long way uses a lot of fuel to transport it whereas local producers use very little fuel. Using fuel is bad for our planet because it makes gases that damage the atmosphere and we should be using locally grown food wherever possible.

I' ve drawn a tomato. It came from Holland.

Talk about locally produced foods. What grows in your area? Ask volunteers to tell about any food that their parents grow in their gardens. Do any have allotments? Explain what allotments are and that in olden times the landowners would allow villagers a small piece of land to grow food for their families. Are organic vegetables better for us? Where do you get them?

Explain about farmers' markets. Are there any in your locality? Who visits them and what kinds of things do people buy there? Ask the children to tell you what they know about farmers' markets. Explain about vegetable boxes; the scheme whereby growers make up boxes of vegetables, usually locally grown, to be delivered to people's houses.

Ask the children to bring in some labels from food containers that their parents have bought. Normally the country of origin is written on the bag or box. In Circle Time, sort these into 'local' and 'abroad'. Make a list of the foods from abroad and the country of origin. Match the countries with your global map to find out which travels the furthest. Ask each child to choose one food to draw and write the country of growth near it. Display these around your world map.

This would be a good opportunity to grow some salads in your classroom or in a pot outside. Record the growing, seeding and harvesting of the crop and arrange a tasting celebration.

http://www.coolkidsforacoolclimate.com/Causes&Effects/FoodMiles.htm.

Environmental issues – older children

Food miles

Explain what food miles are and that damage to our planet is caused by fuel used in transporting it. Explain that a food's country of origin may be on the label, but it's often impossible to tell how far the food has travelled and by what means. The means of transport, as well as the distance travelled, are important to consider. A long journey by boat has less environmental impact than a shorter one by road. Milk or potatoes can be transported many miles to be packaged at a central depot and then sent many miles back to be sold near where they were produced in the first place.

Ask the children to work in pairs to write a list of foods they eat that could never be produced in this country. Ask them to write down a second list of all the foods that could be produced locally. How many of these foods are also on the first list? Read through their lists and discuss whether we should restrict our foods to those that we can grow here. For example, should we be eating apples from New Zealand in spring and summer or should we eat only our own crops of apples in autumn and winter? Freshly picked fruit and vegetables not only have more taste, they are also better nutritionally. Can they explain what 'organic' means?

Ask the children to work in small groups to design a poster with an eye-catching slogan urging people to eat locally produced foods whenever possible. Vote on the best one or two to display and promote.

Learning at home

Group the children into three groups to investigate breakfast, lunch or supper. Ask each child to enlist the help of parents in collecting a whole day's packaging of the food they eat at that meal.

Back in school, ask the children to work with the rest of their group to find out how far their whole meal has travelled. Ask them to draw and write about their meal. Collect each meal's data on one sheet to display and discuss. Where has the food come from? Which meals have travelled the fewest food miles? How far in total have all the foods travelled?

Read the story to the children and then carry out the activities below.

Cidhina's new toy

Cidhina lives in South America in a country called Brazil. The largest city is Rio de Janeiro, famous all over the world for its beautiful beaches and its carnival, held every year.

Life in the countryside, where Cidhina lives, is quite different. The Amazon rainforest is disappearing, together with its wildlife, because so many trees have been cut down. There is a lake nearby. The village in summer is hot, dusty and dry. It isn't always so. Half the year it is dry and dusty and the other half it rains! The houses are made of earth and they line each side of the one dirt road that goes through the village. Although Cidhina's family has a television set, the electricity supply is weak, and there are power cuts nearly every day.

All the children of the village have to work hard to help their parents but when work is done they love to play games together, sometimes football or a skipping game called elastico. Sometimes they go swimming. They don't have many toys.

Cidhina has been ill but she is now getting better and her friends want to make her a toy for a present. They don't know what to make. They look at all the things around them, they explore a rubbish tip nearby to see if there is anything there and find an old and broken down rusty bike left behind when one family moved to the city of Rio. The children look at the bike; the frame is bent and twisted, no use at all, but the front wheel is almost round with a torn, flat tyre.

One of Cidhina's friends looks at the wheel and says, 'Are you thinking what I'm thinking?' His brother nods and says, 'Yes, a hoop'. They both go to their father and speak to him quietly; they ask him if he would help them to take the wheel out of the bike frame so that they can make a hoop. Of course he will; he does this straight away and the two boys go off with the wheel. They take off the old ruined tyre and take away the tape that they find around the metal of the wheel, replacing it with strips of fabric to cover the sharp spoke ends. They straighten all the spokes that are bent and take a good look at it. It is rather rusty, but they rub the rust on the rim with sand until it is smooth and then go to ask grown-ups if they can find some paint. Yes, they are given a small, half empty tin of red paint and paint the rim. When it is finished, they tie strips of fabric to some of the spokes near the hub to decorate it. It is, truly, a good hoop. They try it out. It runs well.

When they give the toy to Cidhina, she is really pleased. She smiles and goes outside her house to try it out. Soon all the children are playing with the hoop, taking turns. 'You are clever, you two,' she says 'We can all play with this'.

Activities

In Circle Time, talk about the story and how Cidhina felt when she was given the hoop. Ask them to think how each child felt when:

- the brothers made the hoop
- the brothers gave it to Cidhina
- Cidhina shared it with all the other children.

Ask the children to think about making toys from recycled materials. What kinds of things could they make? Set groups of older children the challenge of making a toy or game from recycled materials.

Ask them to think about the last-time they had a new toy. Was it bought from a shop or was it made as Cidhina's toy was? Ask them to finish the sentence.

'My last new toy was a ...'

Were they as pleased as Cidhina?

Ask the children to draw a picture of Cidhina and her friends playing with the hoop and to write a sentence about it.

Ask the children to write a story about someone else who needed some warm clothes, how this came about and what the person felt about it.

Debate the difference between needing something and wanting something. Ask them to think about whether they need anything now and if so, what they need. Do we, in this country, actually need things or do we just want things?

Ask them to finish either sentence:

'I need this because ...'

or

'I want this because ...'

Environmental Issues – Reflection

In Circle Time, discuss all the environmental issues in this section and read any displays the children have made. Ask them to look through their Global Citizenship folders, read the work there and add to the list of children they have worked with. What do they remember most about each section? Can they think of other areas of the environment that you have not discussed? If so, now is the time to talk about these other issues, for instance, fly-tipping, disposal of atomic waste and waste we send to other countries or other countries send to us for disposal. Do they know that old fridges need de-gassing and that old mobile phones can be recycled or sent to developing countries?

Ask them to think about children who live in less developed countries with their different environments. Have any of the children visited such places? If so, ask them to tell you about them. Remind the children that we throw away a lot of things that people in other countries would like to have. Do they know that if their families take old medicines and tablets back to the chemist, there is a scheme to send useful ones to other countries? Do they know that if they take old spectacles to the optician, there is a scheme to send these out to other countries where people are in need of them?

Ask them to remember not to waste water by turning off the taps when they have sufficient in a bowl and taking a short shower instead of a full bath.

Ask the children to work together to make a class picture similar to the drawing at the beginning of this section entitled *This Wonderful World*. Can they think of any more speech bubbles to add?

Getting involved

Ask the children if they can think of any ways that they can help the environment in this country. What can they themselves actually do? Ask each child to write a note of intent so that they will not forget their responsibilities.

Global challenges

Can they think of any ways in which they can help the environment in other countries? Does our government help? What could it do to help keep the world-wide environment safer? Can children in your class do anything?

Do you use water wisely?   Tick one column ✓

	always	some- times	never
Is your washing machine full before you use it?			
Do you run your washing machine when it is not full?			
Do you wash vegetables under a running tap?			
Do you use a bowl for cleaning vegetables?			
If a tap drips, do you tell your family and get it fixed?			
Do you have a bath every day?			
Do you share bathwater with someone?			
Do you shower every day?			
Do you leave the tap running when you clean your teeth?			
Has your toilet got a short and a long flush?			
Has your toilet got a 'save a litre' bag to reduce water use?			
Do you use a hosepipe to water plants?			
Do you use a watering can from an outside tap?			
Do you have a water butt?			

Compare your answers with a friend. Which of you is most careful with water?

Can you see where you can save water in the future?

Litter grid

This litter was found in a beauty spot. Some will break down and rot quickly; others will take a long time. Some are not safe; some are so dangerous that even an adult will need to take care. Tick the column that you think tells what to do.

Type of litter	This will quickly degrade.	This will take a long time to degrade.	These are dangerous – tell a grown-up.	Don't ever touch these – tell a grown-up.
crisp packet				
paper bag				
drink can				
syringe				
plastic bag				
half a beefburger				
bandage with blood				
fishing line and hook				
old T-shirt				
polystyrene container				
half a brick				
broken glass				
open sardine tin				
sweet wrapper				
dog mess				
old shoe				
newspaper				

On the back of the paper, write what you think the owner should have done with each item instead of throwing it away in the beauty spot.

Section 3

Fairness

Focus

This section will help children to think about how things can be fair or unfair in this country, in other developed countries and developing countries by exploring various issues such as:

- gender issues
- inclusion
- persecution
- racism and children from different cultures
- respect
- rules
- valuing and respecting difference.

Remind the children to keep their Global Citizenship folder up to date by putting into it any work they do in this section.

See the activity sheets 'Who does what?' 'A garden for everyone', 'Can you help Rashid?' and 'Rules in different places' at the end of this section.

You may find the following website informative.

http://street-children.org.uk/colombia.htm

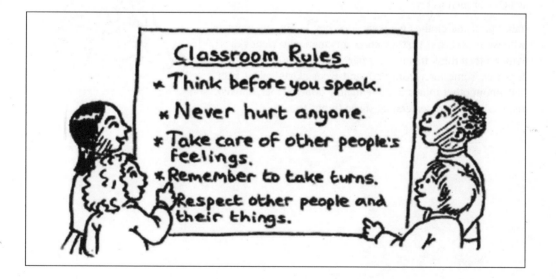

Fairness – younger children

Gender issues

Talk with the children about fairness and being fair. Explain that today you are thinking about whether things are fair to boys and girls equally. Talk first about the kinds of games they like to play and whether boys and girls like to play the same games and play with the same toys.

> Do boys and girls like to play the same things?
> 15 of us think they do
> 12 of us think they don't.

Find out whether they think that boys and girls like to play the same things by asking those who think they do to stand up and count themselves. Ask some of the children who don't think this to justify their responses.

Explain that years ago most women stayed at home to look after the house and their family and that only the men went out to work. Ask volunteers to say what they think about that and whether it was fair.

Talk about the old saying 'Pink for a little girl and blue for a boy'. Do any girls wear blue clothes and do any boys wear pink? Do they think the old saying was gender stereotyping?

Ask the children to draw a grown-up person crying. Ask them to say whether this is a man or a woman and why they are crying. Count up the numbers of men and women drawn. Did the girls draw women and the boys draw men or did more of the children draw women crying? Talk about the results of their drawings and ask them whether they think it's OK for men to cry.

This is a lady crying. She is very sad. Men cry too sometimes.

Talk about the clothes we wear. Do they know any women who wear trousers? Do they know any men who wear skirts? Why do they think this is? Is it fair? Talk about this and why it is that some men from Scotland wear skirts called kilts. Talk about other things that are mainly done by men and ask them whether women can do these things too.

Fairness – older children

Gender issues

Talk to the children about the differences between men and women in the workplace. Are men more suited to some jobs than others? Are there some jobs that are mainly done by men and some mainly done by women? Why is this? Is this always the case?

Talk about fairness between boys and girls. Do children expect boys and girls to behave differently in various situations? Do boys and girls have different standards of behaviour? Is this fair?

Ask the children to consider and debate these statements:

Boys are stronger than girls or girls are weaker than boys.
Girls are the equal of boys.
Boys are treated differently than girls.
More is expected of boys than girls or vice versa.
Girls need to be looked after by boys or vice versa.
Grown-ups treat girls differently to boys.
Girls and their friends are closer than boys and their friends.

Ask each child to choose one of the above statements and write what they think, giving their reasons. Use the activity sheet 'Who does what?' at the end of this section. Discuss their gender choices and any link to their own gender.

Ask the children to think about men and women. Do they think that men have a different role at home? Do men and women have different responsibilities at home? Who makes the decisions? How is this decided? Is this always fair?

Learning at home

Ask the children to find out the roles of men and women in other countries, for example, who carries the water, who carries the wood, who earns the money, who cooks the food? What are boys allowed to do that girls are not? Why do more boys than girls go to school? Why and at what age do they drop out of school? Ask the children to question 'Is it fair?'.

Fairness – younger children

Inclusion

In Circle Time, talk with the children about inclusion and what it means. Tell them that it is important to include children in their games, in their work and in the general activities in the classroom. Explain that excluding people, deliberately keeping them out and not letting them join in, is a kind of bullying.

Ask the children to think of not being allowed to join in and to raise a fist if this has happened to them. Ask volunteers to talk about how they felt when this happened.

Explain that there are times when they will not be allowed to join in things. Ask the children to think about a time when they have not been allowed to do something for a very good reason. Can volunteers say when this happened to them? Ask the children to draw a picture of a time when someone couldn't join in some activity for a very good reason. Share their pictures and discuss the reasons.

> *I couldn't go on the canal picnic because my mum said I was too young to go by the water.*

Remind the children that all people are equal even when they do not look the same or behave the same. Explain that it is only fair for everyone to have equal chances of doing things and talk about your classroom organisation for ensuring that you are fair to all the children there.

Tell this story:

> A family moved to a different part of this country to work and live. They spoke differently from their new neighbours and ate different kinds of food as they were vegetarians. They tried to be friendly with the people in their new neighbourhood but the neighbours were not friendly back. Some of the people at the man's work laughed at him because he spoke differently. In the shops, his wife felt uncomfortable because she was different.

What do the children think of this story? Is it fair? What would they do if they were grown-ups there? If a child in this family came to their school, would they include him or her in their work and play? Ask the children to draw this incoming family and say what they would do if they were the neighbours.

Fairness – older children

Inclusion

Talk to the children about exclusion and inclusion. Help them to understand the fairness of inclusion and the unfairness of exclusion. Remind them that, as citizens of this country, we are all equal and deserve the same treatment. Talk about children with disabilities and special needs. Some of these children used always to go to special kinds of schools. Nowadays many are integrated into normal schools with special help. Debate the advantages and disadvantages of this.

Talk about how people usually welcome new neighbours. What kinds of things do they often do to make sure that they feel happy and welcome? Talk about how these new neighbours would feel if they were not included in the local community. Ask the children to finish the sentence:

'They would feel ...'

Make a list of these feelings.

Discuss the following scenarios, and how people can be included:

- the first day of a new child in their class
- being fair to someone they don't really like much
- letting someone join in their group
- how to explain that she cannot join in at once, but that later she can
- how to include someone in a wheelchair in their games
- how to include someone when others in the group don't want them.

Unless inappropriate, use the activity sheet 'How can you help Rashid?'

Talk to the children about other countries where things are not fair. In some of the developing countries, the people do not have enough food, clothes, water or somewhere to live. Sometimes older children cannot go to school because they have to work. Sometimes even young children have to work to help the family to buy enough food to live. Sometimes they are sick and there are no hospitals or doctors to help them. Sometimes they have illnesses that will kill them and there are no drugs to help.

Learning at home

Ask the children to find out from newspapers, the Internet and their families about the money that people donate to help a developing country. What will the money buy and how much will pay for one thing? Ask the children to write one item and its cost in a speech bubble to discuss at school before making a display.

Fairness – younger children

Persecution

Explain to the children what persecution is. Use a Bible story such as 'The Good Samaritan' or the Israelites' flight to talk about races that were persecuted in the past. Tell the children that this kind of thing is happening today; some peoples of the world are persecuted by others. Read this story.

Mihai is seven years old and he lives with his parents and two sisters in Romania. His father is a Romanian gypsy musician and they travel around the countryside with other musical gypsy families. Mihai would like to live in a house or even just stay in one place to live so that he could make friends. His family doesn't stay in one place long enough for him to get used to going to school so he is finding it hard to read and write. When he does go to school other children are unkind to him because he doesn't know what to do. They laugh at him and call him names.

Some adults in Romania are very unkind to gypsies and persecute them. People who are settled and live in houses don't want gypsies in their town, parking on the spare bits of land and making a mess there. The government won't find them anywhere to camp so they have to keep on travelling around. Some of Mihai's family went to Germany to try to escape the racial persecution but many were sent back. People in Germany didn't want them there either.

Mihai is happy in his new camp with his family.

There used to be a King of Romania but he was forced out of the country in 1947 and came to England. Some of the Romanian people would like to have a king again because they think he would rule them more fairly.

(See website http://www.pixton.org/TomsRomaniaGypsyPage.html)

Discuss the feelings of persecuted people like Mihai and his family.

Ask your class how they would feel if:

- they had no settled home?
- their families were persecuted?
- they couldn't go to school?
- people didn't like them and tried to hurt them?

Ask the children to draw a picture of Mihai and his family and to write about how he feels.

Fairness – older children

Persecution

Before the lesson, bring into the classroom any news items of persecution at home or abroad. Talk about the meanings of the word 'persecution' and make a list of the different words that can be used instead. Explain that persecution can vary from being unkind to someone who is different, keeping them out of games, not making them feel welcome in our community to physically hurting or even killing people whom we don't like for some reason or other.

harassment

maltreatment

bullying

singling out

hounding

harrying

discrimination

prejudice

intolerance

inequality

Ask the children to supply examples of persecution in this country and go through your newspaper cuttings for any kind of discrimination or bullying in this country for discussion. Ask the children to think of solutions and discuss whether they will work.

Talk about slavery and how African people were collected from their own country and sold as slaves in this and other countries. Discuss with the children how they would feel if they were stolen from their parents and taken to a new country to be made into slaves.

Now think of discrimination in other countries. Are some people forced to flee from their homeland? Are some people not allowed to worship the God of their choice? Why and how do people become refugees?

Discuss the present situation. What wars are going on at present? Which people are made to flee? How do people in this country help those who have to flee their homeland? Do we help them or do we keep them out of this country? Can we help them to stay in their own country and be safe?

Learning at home

Ask the children to talk with their families and to look in newspapers or on the Internet for examples of persecution. Discuss all these issues and explain that there will be no solution until we all become tolerant of other people's rights and beliefs and accept that we all have the right to our place in the world.

Fairness – younger children

Racism and children from different cultures

Look at your global map and identify some of the countries. Explain that all these countries have people of different races with different ways of living and likes and dislikes. Talk about how these various people look different from others – different colour of skin, kinds of hair, colours of eyes and bone structure. Remind the children that all people in the world have the right to be equal; no one race or culture is better than another.

If you are fortunate in having children from various races and cultures in your class or school, ask them to tell you of their ways of living. How do they keep alive their own beliefs and traditions while living in this country? What are their traditions?

Use storybooks to learn about the lives of people living in other countries and choose positive images of these people to help the children understand the beauty and breadth of their lives, their customs and traditions.

Talk about how it used to be many years ago when people mainly stayed in their own country and visited but rarely went to live in other countries. Remind the children about the story *No Two Zebras are the Same* and that we are all different and special.

Explain that the colour of our skin is inherited from our parents and that all skins are slightly different shades whether black, brown or white. Ask the children to examine their own and other children's skin with a magnifying glass, to draw the magnified skin and write about how skins vary.

If your school has a predominance of one cultural or racial group, you could explore the possibility of finding a link to a school in this country where there are children of various races. Set up a two-way dialogue with this school and encourage the children to find out about the different lives of the children in both schools.

I am with Jamal who comes from Pakistan. We are both different and good friends.

Fairness – older children

Racism and children from different cultures

Look at and choose some of the activities for younger children as a starter. Explain just what racism is and that it means discriminating or showing prejudice against people of a different race or culture.

Talk about how the human race has adapted to the environment over thousands of years. People who live in very high altitudes where there is less oxygen in the air can live and work there more easily than people who come from low altitudes. Their bodies are more efficient at using the available oxygen. People in hot countries developed a skin that could cope with the sun; those in cold places developed skins to cope with the cold. Man has adapted to the environment and the best body for that environment developed. Explain that people in some countries have developed skills, knowledge and technology faster than others and that no one knows why this is.

Ask the children to work in pairs and to choose a country from your world map to investigate. Using books and the internet, ask them to find out about the ways, employment, customs, religion, traditions and celebrations of the people in that country. Ask them to find out about the geography and history of the people there and to write about their findings. Ask them each to write a story about how a person from that country might feel if they came to this country to live. Would they be able to find work that they could do? Would they find other people of their race to be with? Would they adapt to this environment easily?

Make sure that the children understand that all people are equal, that it is against human rights to discriminate against anyone because of their race.

Learning at home

Ask the children to look through national newspapers at home, cut out and bring to school any references to racism or discrimination. Use these real-life cases for discussion, emphasising that all people are equal. Explain that we must try to understand other people's ways or customs even if we don't agree with them and that it is against human rights and the law to discriminate against anyone for any reason.

Fairness – younger children

Respect

Ask the children to tell you what they think 'respect' means and make a list of the words they offer. Explain that it means looking up to people, listening to their opinions, taking notice of what people say, thinking about how they feel, being polite and well mannered, obeying instructions. Talk to the children about obeying adults and doing as they say. It may help the children to understand if you ask them to give you examples of disrespect, for example, answering back, shouting at, being insolent or rude.

Ask the children to draw a picture of themselves being respectful to someone in their family. How will they show this? Share the pictures and what the children have written. Talk about the different voices and words we use to different people. Can volunteers demonstrate how they talk to various people?

Talk about respecting people outside their family, people in authority in school and the wider community. Talk about respecting the rules of your school and classroom.

Explain that we should respect the laws of the land because these have been made by people to help all people to know the right things to do.

Talk about respecting each other and remind the children that we are all different and entitled to our own opinions but at the same time we have to respect other people's opinions.

Go around the circle, asking the children to finish this sentence:

'I like … but you don't have to like the same thing.'

Go around the circle with this sentence to finish:

'You like … and I respect that.'

Talk about how people in other cultures show respect – some by putting hands together, bowing or kneeling; taking shoes off before going into a sacred building. Use a drama session to explore different ways of showing respect. Ask children to volunteer to demonstrate, and others to guess, where they are and to whom they are showing respect.

Fairness – older children

Respect

As with younger children, ask your class to tell you what they think the word 'respect' means. Talk about self-respect and respecting others; manners and honesty, with examples such as, jumping a queue, using a mobile phone loudly, giving up a seat, holding a door open, dropping litter, saying 'please' and 'thank you', handing in things they might find. Ask them to give their examples of children and young people showing respect to adults and people in authority. Remind them that it is often not what they say but how they say it and the body language they convey. In Circle Time, ask volunteers to show how they would speak and act towards various people; for example, how would they ask a friend to tea; how would they ask their granny?

Ask the children to think about how we show respect towards people in our religion; in school prayers we bow our heads, in some places of worship people kneel. Ask volunteers to say how other people show respect towards their religious leaders, for example, some people touch their forehead as a sign of respect, bow, or put their hands together and bow.

Talk about the kinds of clothes they wear, for example, a hat – do people wear one or do they take it off? People in the services salute an officer. Gentlemen used to take off their hats and bow to ladies. Ladies used to curtsey and they still do when meeting the Queen. Some people cover their heads or take off their shoes. Some wear a special colour, for example, only queens of Roman Catholic countries should appear before the Pope dressed in white.

Ask the children to think about showing respect on various occasions and work in pairs to practise showing this respect. Ask volunteers to demonstrate and explain what they do and how this shows they are respecting someone.

Learning at home

Ask the children to find out ways that people in other races, cultures or countries show respect to each other and to those in authority. Ask each child to make a zigzag book or a four-page, folded booklet with each page describing and illustrating different ways of showing respect.

Fairness – younger children

Rules

Remind the children about what they have already learned about respecting the rules of your school.

Talk about the rules you have for your classroom and for Circle Time. Ask the children to tell you some of them. Do you have different rules for different places in school: rules for the dining room, rules for the playground, rules for the library? Talk about these rules; explain why we need to have them and who made them.

Our good rule is...
Don't hurt
people's feelings.

Ask the children to think of one really good rule for your classroom – a rule to keep everyone safe and happy. Write down their responses and from these, try to make up one good rule that everyone thinks is fair.

Talk about the rules in their homes and ask for examples. Help them to see that these rules are to make sure that things are fair to everyone.

Talk about the rules outside school; rules for the swimming pool, for the gym, for the football pitch. Talk about rules in the wider community – road safety rules, rules about waiting your turn in a queue, not dropping litter. Ask the children to illustrate one of these rules and make a display of their pictures.

Explain that making rules is a democratic process and that people of the country are responsible for making the rules or laws of the country. Can the children give you any examples of laws, for example, not walking on grass in special areas, keeping dogs out of shops, driving on the left?

Ask the children to think of just one of these laws and draw two pictures, one of people keeping the law and one of people breaking the law. Ask them to tell you how they would feel if they broke that law, how other people would feel, what could happen if everybody broke that law.

Fairness – older children

Rules

Explain that rules and laws are made to make sure that everything is fair for everybody. If we all keep the rules and laws, everyone is happy; if we break them, things happen to cause problems, unhappiness or danger.

Ask the children to think of some games they know. Ask volunteers to tell you the rules of some of them. Talk about what would happen to games such as football, tennis or cricket if people didn't keep to the rules. Ask the children to complete the activity sheet 'Rules for different places'.

Talk with the children about the democratic principle of making and keeping laws. Explain that in olden times the village elders would make rules and these would apply to the people in that village. Some were made a long time ago because of the way that people lived then. Newer laws have been made as people's lives have changed. Ask for examples of new laws, such as hosepipe bans to save water, computer hacking, immigration and smoking in public places.

Ask the children to think of laws or rules that apply to them in the area where they live. Ask them to tell you what these laws are about and make a list of headings, for example, community areas, garden waste, parks and gardens, litter, dogs. Ask children to work in pairs, choose one heading from the list and write their own laws about it, laws that would help to make and keep their locality a safe, happy and fair place for everyone.

Talk to the children about developing countries where things are not always fair. Ask children to work in groups to identify some catastrophe in a mythical country which has left the people in need. Ask them to make a list of rules to make sure that different kinds of aid would be distributed fairly.

Learning at home

Your area will have written bylaws for everyone to see. Over a weekend, ask the children to find out, by talking to people, using the library, by phone or from the Internet the bylaws in place in the area where you live. Ask them to list the section headings and to copy down the penalty for anyone breaking these bylaws.

Fairness – younger children

Valuing and respecting difference

Remind the children about work done on 'Similarities and differences' (p. 9).

Remind the children that though we humans are all the same, in so many ways we all are different, special and unique. Talk about children from other cultures; find and use storybooks where children have different-coloured skin, eyes and hair. If possible draw on the experiences of the class, identifying differences in culture. If this is not possible invite somebody into the classroom who can provide a different perspective.

Remind the children about the word 'respect' and what it means. Ask the children to tell you what they think it means and add to their knowledge with your explanations, for example, respecting people means think well about them, accept them as they are, think about their feelings, be polite to them, even if they look very different, have different ways and different customs. Explain to the children that it is really important to respect the fact that we are all different and that we bring something of ourselves to our school and wider community. Ask them to think about this story.

James went to live in India because his Dad got a job there. There was a school for English children for him to go to and he met many English children there. Around his home there were many Indian children who went to a different school; they knew lots of things about India that James didn't know. They knew some words of English and they talked to James and told him many things but often talked to each other in their own language. James thought they were very clever and he tried to learn their language. The Indian children helped him by telling him names of things in the house and he could soon talk to them quite a bit. He found out about their homes, their games and the things they did at home. When James's parents found out that he was playing with the local children, they were not best pleased. They said that James should only play with children from the English-speaking school. This made James sad because he thought that if they could all talk and play together they would respect each other more.

Ask the children to tell you if they think James was right – or his parents. Ask them to draw a picture of James and the other children playing and learning about each other and to write a sentence about their picture.

Fairness – older children

Valuing and respecting difference

Remind the children about work done on 'Similarities and differences' (p. 10).

In Circle Time, explain to the children the importance of respecting and valuing the differences of people from different races, cultures and countries. Ask them to say what 'respecting the differences' and 'valuing the differences' mean and ask them to give examples of how we show that we do this.

Remind them that we all have a lot to learn about people from different backgrounds. Ask them to think of how we can show that we respect and value people who come from different races, cultures or countries.

Read the story about James from the previous page to the children. Talk about how children often find it easier than adults to accept and value friends who come from different backgrounds. Ask them to write their own feelings about James and his parents.

Talk about any stories you have read in class where children work and play with children who are different to them. Discuss the kinds of things that children will find difficult to accept in a new country. Ask them to write a story about someone who goes to live in another country and how they fit in there.

I think that James was right to be friends to the local children. He could learn lots about the country and the way people live there. By making friends with all kinds of people we can show that we value them all as our friends.

Learning at home

Explain that people are 'different' in other ways as well as due to race and culture. Some people have health conditions or disabilities. Ask them to find out about the lifestyle of someone like this who has a good life even with their condition or disability. Sometimes being 'different' can be a challenge and spur people to do great things. Ask them to draw and write about this person. Share this work with the rest of the class. Remind them that we are all as we are because of our family genes; we must also respect and value ourselves.

Read the story to the children and then carry out the activities below.

Read the fact sheet about albinism after the Reflection.

Madelizo's story

In Africa, a baby boy was born, his parents called him Madelizo. His mother was black, his father was black but their baby's skin was white. When he was born his parents were very shocked at the colour of his skin. His father walked a long way to the hospital to see a doctor who told him that this was very rare. Sometimes if both parents have a certain gene there is a very, very small chance that a child will be born an albino. It had not happened there before.

Because of his white skin, Madelizo's parents had to be very careful about going out with him in the sun. His skin did not have protection against the sun and if he got sunburned he could easily develop a kind of skin cancer. So Madelizo had to stay indoors during the day and only went outside during the early morning or evening when there was little sunshine. Madelizo was very much loved by his parents; he was their child and they loved to care for him. His mother kept him clean and gave him sensible clothes to wear; she made good food for him, cuddled him and showed that she loved him. His father also loved him, talking to him and playing with him.

He was not loved outside his home though, because the neighbours and other children were scared because he was so different. They didn't want to acknowledge him. He was different, not at all like them. He could never be one of them. He didn't belong. Some of the neighbours thought that Madelizo was bad because of his white skin; they just couldn't understand why he was white so they wouldn't accept him, just because he was not the same as them.

Other children in the village were the same. They did as their parents did. They wouldn't touch him or play with him so poor Madelizo had no friends at all. He had no one to play with; no one to share his games.

Madelizo's parents were worried that when he grew up he would find school difficult. They knew that other boys in his class might ignore him, tease him or be unkind. That would make it hard for him to fit in.

When he was almost five years old, Madelizo's mother visited the village school to talk to the teacher. The school building was old and falling down with a leaking roof and so the lessons for the 90 children took place outside in the shade of a large baobab tree. She explained that Madelizo mustn't be outside in the sun but even the teacher didn't seem to understand.

Ask the children what they think about this story. Is it fair? Ask them to think about these questions:

* What do they think could happen when Madelizo started school?
* Would he be able to stay indoors for his lessons?
* What would happen if he had to be in the sun all day?
* Would the other children be fair to him?
* Would other parents want their children to exclude Madelizo from their play?

- How could the children include him?
- What could they say and do?

Activities

Ask the children to think about how Madelizo would feel at school with no friends. What could he do if no one would play with him? How would he feel as he grew up?

Ask the children to think of a good ending to this story. Perhaps someone else could be in the story to talk to the teacher to help her to understand. Perhaps someone else could be in the story and help Madelizo.

Ask younger children to draw a picture of a good ending and to write or copy a sentence about it. Ask older children to write their own good ending. They can put themselves in the story if they like and think about what they could do to help Madelizo to fit in and be happy at school and home.

In Circle Time, talk about how children get excluded in this country. What kinds of things make some children want to exclude others? How does it make excluded children feel? How can we make sure this doesn't happen?

With older children, talk about adults who get excluded in this country. How can we stop this happening?

Fairness – Reflection

In Circle Time, set up a general discussion about fairness; include all the ways life can be fair or unfair depending on the circumstances. Talk about your rules for fairness in the classroom. Ask the children to tell you some ways that people and the government in this country try to make sure that everything is fair for everyone. Talk about some countries where this doesn't happen.

Ask the children to look through their Global Citizenship folders, read the work there and add to the list of children they have worked with. Has any child worked with all the children in the class yet? What do they remember most about each section? Can they think of other ways in which people are fair – or are unfair? Talk about these and what they and grown-ups could do about it.

Can they think of any ways in which girls and boys are not treated the same? Ask them what they are going to do about this. Remind them of their own responsibility to be fair, both at school and at home as well as in the wider community. Talk again about respect, both to people in school and at home. Remind them of the importance of treating people who are different from them with respect and that they can make them feel valued in our community.

Remind them that rules are there to help us to make things fair for everyone and of their own part in keeping to the rules.

Getting involved

Ask the children to think whether there is anything that they can do to help to make sure that their world is a fairer place for everyone. Are there people that can help, for example, charities to help people with health conditions? Is there anything that they can do to help these charities?

Global challenges

Remind the children that life for people in other parts of the world is not always fair and that some people are treated without respect and are not valued. Can they think of anything that they could do to help to make things fairer? Can they think of things that they could do, or help to get done when they are older and have some power? Is giving money enough?

Fact sheet: Albinism, by Brenda Zea

Most people have a very biased and stereotyped view of people with albinism. Many see albinos as persons with white hair, white skin and red eyes. This is a common myth that has perpetuated itself because the truth about albinism is not widely known. One in 17,000 people in the United States has a form of albinism. There are many different types of albinism, depending on the amount of melanin in a person's eyes. While some people have red or violet colored eyes, most have blue eyes. Even fewer have hazel, brown or gray eyes. These discrepancies between reality and the red-eyed albino myth are the reason that most albinos do not even realize that they have a form of albinism.

The two most common types of albinism are Type-1 albinism which affects hair, skin and eye color and Type 2 which affects mostly the eyes, but the skin and hair may have slight discoloration. Most albinos have serious vision difficulties and many are considered legally blind, or have such poor eyesight that they must use intensive prescription bifocals. A few, however, have good enough visual acuity to drive a car. Those with rare forms of albinism can experience problems with bruising, bleeding, and susceptibility to diseases that affect the bowels and lungs or can develop other physical problems in addition to their eyes; their life span is not as long as other albinos' lives. If an albino person spends too much time out in the sun (this occurs mostly in albinos from tropical countries) they can develop skin cancer. While most of these cancers are treatable, they can only be treated if the facilities are available. Fortunately albinism is not very common in most cultures because it is either caused by a rare recessive gene (this requires both parents to carry the gene in order for you to be albino), or an even rarer case, in which albinism is caused by genetic mutation. As it is such a rare occurrence, albino people are often met with hostility and misunderstanding. Often they are teased at school and find it hard to fit in, especially when the child is from a normally dark-skinned race – they stand out from their peers. A real eye-opener for the entire country came when in 1998, Rick Guidotti published a photo-journal in the June edition of *Life* magazine. He was one of the first people to portray albinos as normal, fashionable people. While this helped the albino community a little, old stereotypes still thrive even in modern culture.

Abridged from http://serendip.brynmawr.edu/biology/b103/f02/web1/bzea.html

Who does what?

Draw a person carrying out appropriate activities for each job

My name is ....

1. a taxi driver	2. a nurse	3. a doctor
4. a solicitor	5. a gardener	6. a teacher
7. a builder	8. a painter	9. a plumber

On the other side of your paper, say whether each person is a man or woman and why you chose that gender for each occupation. Write what you would like to do when you are grown up and why.

78

A garden for everyone

Design an environmentally friendly public garden for everyone in the community including those who have a disability, specific health condition or use a wheelchair.

On the back of this paper make a list of everything you would put in such a garden. Put a ring around things on your list that are good for the environment.

Can you help Rashid?

Read the story and answer the questions.

Rashid is nine years old and has been watching the news. It is about terrorist activities and people killing other people in a country far away. Some people blame the Muslims and this makes Rashid angry and sad. He is a Muslim himself and feels anxious about this. His parents had fled their homeland about 20 years ago and he has been born and brought up in this country and is British. Rashid is upset about the terrorism but more upset about going to school tomorrow; he is the only Muslim in the class, everyone else is white, and he thinks that some of the other children might blame him because he is different to them and because of the terrorism.

How do you think Rashid would be feeling as he walks to school the next day?
I think he would be feeling ...

What would you say to Rashid about the terrorism?
I would say ...

What would you say to Rashid about being a Muslim?
I would say ...

What could you do and say to make Rashid feel better about looking different from other children in the class?
I could ...

What could you do to help Rashid feel included in the classroom?
I could ...

On the other side, write about what you and your friends could do to make sure that Rashid feels OK about being in your class and school.

80

Rules in different places

Draw each place and write a good rule for each place. Turn over the paper and do some more.

School playground	Public library
Bus stop	Swimming pool
Country park	Riverbank

Section 4

Exploring various cultures

Focus

This section will help children to learn how people from different cultures lead their lives, with particular emphasis on:

- who has come from other countries?
- food
- games children play
- toys and fun
- stories
- clothes
- festivals
- music.

Remind the children to keep their Global Citizenship folder up to date by putting into it any work they do in this section.

See the activity sheets 'Harrig', 'A new game' and 'Other countries' at the end of this section.

Exploring various cultures – younger children

Who has come from other countries?

In Circle Time, explain that many people have come from a different country to be in your community, school or class. Ask the children to tell you where they were born or where their parents were born. If you have children who have moved to this country from another country or whose parents or carers were born abroad, ask them to tell you of their experiences of their country of origin.

Encourage the children born here to ask questions and, if they've been abroad, to talk about experiences of countries they've visited. Talk about famous people from other countries who now live in this country – include people in the news, sportsmen and women, TV personalities and film stars.

Explain that many people of different races and cultures are citizens of this country because they were born here and that these people have the same rights and responsibilities as all people born in this country.

Use your local newspaper and select someone who has come from another country to live in this country. Help the children to find out about life in this person's original country and how it differs from this one. Can you invite this person into your school to talk about why they have come to your area and how it is different from the place where they were born?

My doctor came from Pakistan. His face is brown and his brown eyes shine. I am glad that Dr Kazmin came here to be my doctor.

Use the activity sheet 'Harrig' and talk about how to make Harrig welcome in our world.

Talk about the things in this country that would seem strange to people from other countries if they came to live here. Make a list of them. Ask the children to draw pictures of these things to surround your list to make a wall display.

Exploring various cultures – older children

Who has come from other countries?

Give each child the Harrig activity sheet and talk about what they write.

Use your world map or globe and look at the sizes of the different countries. Explain that many people from these countries came to this country to live. Why do the children think this is? (For example, oppression, war, to learn skills.)

Ask the children to tell you of people they know who came from another country to live here. List the countries they come from and find where they are on your map. Discuss with the children why people want to come to this country and whether they are permanent residents or whether they will return to their original country. Talk about the good things that people bring with them when they come to this country, for example, skills, foods, traditions.

Some come to universities and hospitals to learn and practise skills that they will eventually take back to their own country. Discuss whether this is a good thing and whether this country should encourage this.

Talk about other work that some people from abroad do in this country, for example, in hospitals, in factories, on farms. Some people come for a short time to earn money to send back to their country, for example, migrant workers who come to work on farms in the summer. Discuss how they may feel about the people who live in this country where we seem to have so much, while in their country many have so little.

Ask the children to think of important or famous people who have come to live permanently in this country. Ask them why they think this is and whether they think it is a good thing.

Learning at home

Ask each child to find out about one famous person who came from another country to live here. Ask them to write about what this person does, where they live and why they think they came to live here. Discuss this work in Circle Time and use it to make a wall display to share with others in the school.

Exploring various cultures – younger children

Food

Talk to the children about the foods they like. Make a list of them. Are these all traditional British foods? Draw a ring around the ones that are not and talk about which country that food came from originally. Using your world map or globe, show the children where these countries are and help them to read the names. Ask children who have been on holiday abroad to think of the foods they ate there and to finish this sentence:

'When I was in ... I ate ...'

Explain that many foods we think of as traditionally British originally came from other countries, such as the tomato and potato. Explain that when people from other countries came to live here they brought with them, or tried to find here, the kinds of foods they like to eat. Sometimes they arranged for their favourite foods to be imported. They brought with them recipes for the foods they liked.

My favourite food from another country is Spanish paella.

Talk about different kinds of restaurants – do the children know that people came from other countries to open restaurants in this country? Use your map or globe again to show the children where these countries are.

In Circle Time, ask the children to finish this sentence:

'My favourite food from another country is ...'

Ask each child to draw a picture of their favourite meal that came from another country and to write a sentence about it.

Make a wall display about all the foods they know that come from other countries. Use a world map as the centre and put strings leading from children's pictures of the food to the country.

Talk about feeling hungry – have any of them ever felt really hungry? Explain that children in some countries may not always have enough food to eat. Can they imagine that? How does it make your class feel?

Exploring various cultures – older children

Food

Discuss with the children the kinds of foreign foods that we now take for granted in this country – foods that we consider as our own although they originally came from abroad. Make a list of these, with the country of origin alongside. Using your world map or globe, identify the countries and link the foods to each one. Look at the countries that have no food link. Ask the children to make a list of some of these countries and to find out from books or the Internet one kind of food from each place.

Talk about why people in different countries eat these kinds of foods. It has mainly to do with the availability of the ingredients or the ease of production. Some of them may be of religious significance.

If you have children whose families originate from another country, ask them to talk about the foods from that country that they like to eat. If you can, invite people from different countries into the classroom to talk about the foods they like, the ingredients they use and how they are made. Can you arrange to cook or taste some of these foods?

Talk about the ways we use food for celebration, for birthday parties, picnics and special occasions such as weddings. We have feast days and parties in this country for religious as well as family celebrations. Ask the children to think about how people from all cultures and countries use food as part of fun or celebration and explain that their homework is to be about finding out how people from one country use food as part of fun or celebration.

Talk about people who are short of food, have no choice and would eat any food at all to stop feeling hungry. Can they imagine that?

Learning at home

Ask each child to choose a country from your world map to find out about how people from their chosen country use food for fun or celebration and to produce a short piece of writing and drawing about their findings. Encourage individuals to choose different countries to give you a wide variety of data to discuss afterwards. After discussion, display this work around your world map.

Exploring various cultures – younger children

Games children play

You may like to visit this website before doing these activities:

http://www.gameskidsplay.net/

In Circle Time, tell the children that you are going to try to find out about the games that children play all around the world. Ask them first to think of the games they like to play and to finish this sentence:

'I like to play ...'

Make a list of the games they mention, read it with them before displaying it in the classroom.

I like to play skipping

Ask the children to think about children in other countries – do they think that they will play these games? Will they have the tools to play them, such as balls and skipping ropes? Will they have different games altogether?

The above website lists many games that children all over the world play – several under different names. Try 'Duck Duck Goose Duck' with your children. It's called 'The mush Pot' in Indiana and 'Pesek' in the Czech Republic.

> The children sit down in a circle. One person is 'he' and walks around the outside of the circle, tapping children on the head to say whether they are a duck or a goose. As soon as someone is named a 'goose' they jump up and try to chase 'he'. 'He' tries to run around the circle and sit in the goose's spot before being tapped. If the goose fails, they become 'he'. If the goose succeeds, the original 'he' sits in the centre of the circle and is only released when another person is tagged to take their place.

Talk with the children about international games such as the Commonwealth Games, the Olympics or the football World Cup. Ask each child to ask their families to tell them of a game they used to play when they were a child. Make a book of these games so that the children can play them in playtimes or dinner breaks.

Exploring various cultures – older children

Games children play

You may like to visit the website on the facing page first.

Talk about the games that the children like to play and ask them to help you to make a list of all the games they know. Can you list them under headings, such as 'ball games', 'skipping games', 'ring games', 'tagging games'.

Using the activity sheet 'A new game', ask them to work in pairs to design a board or card game that children in other countries could play.

Explain that variations of many of the games they play are played all over the world, perhaps using different tools or words. For example, in Japan there is a game very similar to badminton that is played on New Year's Day. Japanese children use a 'hagoita' to hit 'hane' and send it to their partner who has to hit it back. The 'hagoita' is made of wood, with a beautiful doll attached to one side. The 'hane' is made of feathers and children hit the 'hane' with the side of the 'hagoita' where there is no doll.

one two three,
it' s not you,
it' s not me,
YOU are he!

On the website there are many games to choose 'he'; they often use fists such as in 'One potato, two potato'. Ask the children to work in pairs to make up their own choosing 'he' rhyme.

Some children in other countries have no money for footballs. Discuss ways to make an object from recycled goods that would make a good football. What would you use and how would you keep it round? Could you make it bounce? Ask children to make something for a game as part of your craft, design and technology at school.

Learning at home

Ask children to do some home research about children's games. Ask them to either write a description of a movement game they have found out about or to invent one that children in any school in any country could play. Talk about these games in school and ask children to write them up for a 'Games Book'.

Exploring various cultures – younger children

Toys

In Circle Time, talk with the children about their toys. Talk about the different kinds of toys such as electronic toys, home-made toys, toys that you move around and use in imaginative play and toys that you just watch. Ask them to finish the sentence:

'My best toy is ...'

Talk about children who live in other countries – does anyone in your class know about the toys that children in other countries like to play with? Explain that many toys were made to help children to learn about the work they would have to do when they are grown–up or to play the roles of the grown-ups in their culture.

Dolls, for example, are played with by children all over the world, though they may not be at all similar to the ones children in this country play with. Playing with dolls can help children to learn how to look after babies. Fighting or war implements are to be found as children's toys in most countries.

Many children in the developing world have toys made from left-over materials that parents use, for example basket dolls and clay models of animals and people. Some are encouraged to practise bead-making skills with clay, painting them before threading them to make necklaces or bracelets.

Most children enjoy dressing up and children from all over the world use and try on clothes belonging to their parents to use in their imaginative role-play games.

Children in Siberia make play houses in the snow. They smooth the walls, inside and out. If the snow is sticky they can make little tables, beds and chairs.

Help your children to make a toy – perhaps a puppet or doll. A simple puppet can be made from a paper bag, the kind with a gusset. If you put your hand inside the upside down bag, the fingers can go in the base to make a face with a movable mouth. Young children can make this into a puppet doll. Challenge older children to make a toy using junk materials, clay or fabrics. Make an exhibition of the finished toys with explanations about how they were made.

Exploring various cultures – older children

Toys

You may like to use the ideas for the younger children on the facing page to set the scene. Explain that some of the developed countries are famous for the toys they make. Germany, for instance, is famous for its ingenious mechanical toys and Steiff teddy bears.

Explain to your class that for many children in towns or cities of developing countries, their toys will be similar to the toys that we have. Where electricity is good they may have computers and electronic games. In rural areas where people are poor, however, toys are a luxury and probably made by themselves or a family adult. They may be simple toys or replicas of artefacts that the grown-ups in their culture use.

The games that these children play will mainly consist of practising skills they will need as they grow up. Many children may not have time to play as we know it in this country; some are set to work at a very early age.

One toy which seems to be fairly universal is the 'buzzer'. This can be made from a circular piece of card about 10 cm in diameter with two holes punched at the centre. String is threaded through the holes and a knot tied to form a loop each side. Children spin the card using the loops of twine before pulling the loops to the sides to make the buzzer spin and make a noise.

Children who live in Ghana play hopscotch. They mark out squares on the ground to play it. Sometimes they make toys and people from clay. They leave them to dry in the sun and then play with them.

Learning at home

Ask the children to research children's toys by using their families, books or the Internet and to find out, draw and describe a toy or game that a child in another country might play with. If it is a child's own made toy, ask them to try to make one to bring to school. Share this work with the whole class and make a display of children's toys from other countries. You may like to separate the toys into those used by children in developing and developed countries.

Exploring various cultures – younger children

Stories

Stories have long been a way of passing family history down the generations. In many cultures, the stories were not written down for many years but transmitted orally through families and village groups. There are many stories to explain how the world began. Most cultures have stories of the beginning of the world. In Circle Time, ask the children to tell you the title of their favourite story by finishing the sentence:

'The story I like best is ...'

Make a list of these. Are they all stories about this country or are some written by authors from other countries?

Talk about the fairy stories of Hans Christian Andersen, the Danish writer who composed *The Ugly Duckling* among others. (See http://hca.gilead.org.il/ for more titles.) Ask the children to look in your book corner and find stories that are written by authors from other countries. Ask them to look through their books at home.

I like the story of 'Amazing Grace'. It's about a black girl called Grace who lives in this country.

Many stories tell about the lives of children in other countries. Make a display of these storybooks from your library and encourage the children to read them. Discuss the lives of children as portrayed in these stories. Do they portray the children's lives as they are today or are they about olden times?

Find stories of myths and legends and talk about the way these stories were written to explain mysteries of the then known world. Talk about Bible stories you have told to the children and explain that these are about the history of Christian people. Talk about stories of other faiths that you have told to the children. Talk about children who live in different countries and what you know about their lives.

Ask the children to draw a picture story of a child who lives in a different country and to write a sentence about the stories that child would like to hear.

Exploring various cultures – older children

Stories

Tell the children that today you are going to learn about stories that children in other countries would know, either from books or told orally by their families. It is said that Russia has one of the best story-telling traditions, with fantastic tales of their heritage. These stories, called *skazki*, were told orally down through the generations and not written down until many years later.

Talk about the troubadours who travelled through old England in the middle ages, telling their stories and singing their songs to the people before moving on to other villages. These people were valued for the stories they told of bravery, daring and fantastic adventures.

In many cultures, stories explained their community's history. Often these stories had a moral theme and were intended to help children to behave in a way that their communities expected.

Make a collection of all the storybooks you have in school about children from other countries. Search the Internet for others. http://www.bolokids.com/2006/0199.htm tells a Russian story of a little snow girl. See http://www.russia-in-us.com/Children/.

Ask the children if any of their parents or families tell them stories of their family's history or other stories. When and how do they do this? Talk about the enjoyment of listening to family stories.

A BBC debate about the decline in story-telling in Africa 2004 – (see http://news.bbc.co.uk/2/hi/africa/3898337.stm) gave comments from people about African stories:

'Friday night Ananse stories were great! Yes I can recall when my auntie "Abuya" will be telling us about Kwaku Ananse the trickster or about the horrors of not being good or of being disobedient. Close by on the charcoal fire, the smells of either ground-nuts toasting or cocoa-yam roasting. We always go to bed either trembling or laughing. Today's youth is missing out on a lot. What a shame!'

Thy-will Koku Amenya, Ghana/USA

Learning at home

Ask the children, with permission from families, to write down an incident in their own lives to tell their children in the future. Ask them to write this down and illustrate it. Display these under the heading of 'Family histories'.

Exploring various cultures – younger children

Clothes

Talk about the clothes that children wear in winter and in summer. Ask the children to tell you why they think these clothes are different. Talk about the need to keep our bodies warm in winter and cool in summer and that the clothes we wear are designed for that reason.

Ask the children to think about the climates of different countries and the kinds of clothing that children will wear in really hot countries and really cold ones. These may only be slightly different versions of the clothes they themselves wear in our different seasons. Most European children wear the same kinds of clothes, although some countries have a national dress, often a peasant skirt and full-embroidered blouse for the girls.

In summer I wear shorts, a T shirt and sandals to keep cool.

Look at your world map or globe and find Rome. Tell the children that in Rome, 2,000 years ago, the boys would wear a tunic down to their knees and a cloak if it was cold. Rich boys would wear a toga with a purple border. Girls would wear a tunic with a woollen belt around their waist.

Look at your world map or globe and find Greece. Here, years ago, people would wear a tunic called a *chiton*. These were made from big squares of cloth held in place by pins at the shoulders and a belt around the waist.

Find Malaysia – here the people wrap themselves in a sarong or loose skirt.

In Middle Eastern countries men and women usually wear flowing robes; while in China, their finest clothes were of rich fabrics embroidered with pearls and jade. In Taiwan, women wore a dress with mandarin collar and slits in the sides of their skirt and Japanese women always used to wear a kimono with socks and wooden clogs. In India women wear saris and sandals.

Help the children to find books with pictures of some of these clothes and ask them to draw one person wearing a different kind of clothes from those we wear.

Exploring various cultures – older children

Clothes

Use information from the facing page to set the scene.

Discuss with the children the various kinds of clothes worn by people living in different countries. Remind them that nowadays many people wear western dress, although some African countries revert to their tribal costumes on special occasions.

The world of fashion dictates what many people wear in all the developed countries as well as in the cities and rich areas of developing countries. It is often in the poorer areas, where people have little money, that they wear any clothes they can find to keep themselves warm and covered. Explain that the charities of western countries have sent clothing to many developing countries and that these clothes may well be the only ones that the people there have.

Ask the children to think about how they would feel if all their clothes were always second hand and they could never have any really new ones.

Many countries have a national dress – a few Welsh, Scottish and Irish children may wear one on very special occasions. In some places, religious beliefs dictate what people wear; women may have their hair and part of their faces covered and wear long skirts; men may wear special hats or caps.

Ask the children to explore all the books you have in school to find out what kinds of traditional clothes people in various countries wear. Ask the children to work in groups of three or four to identify one country and find out the traditional as well as the modern clothing that people there wear. Ask them to draw and write about their findings and then share this with the class.

If you would like to investigate British clothing over the years, this website is helpful: http://schoolweb.missouri.edu/ashland.k12.mo.us/carolee/webpage2.html.

Learning at home

Ask the children to talk to their families, use books and the Internet to find out about any kinds of decoration, hats, head-dresses and or jewellery that people in other countries usually wear with their traditional clothes. Ask them to draw someone wearing these and to write about the occasions when they are worn.

Exploring various cultures – younger children

Festivals

In Circle Time, ask young children to tell you what they think the word 'festival' means. Explain that it can mean a feast or a celebration; it can be a procession or carnival. Ask them to tell you about the festivals they know about and that you have in your area.

Explain that all countries have their own festivals or carnivals and that these are times when people have a holiday and enjoy themselves. Perhaps they know about the Edinburgh Festival, where every year there is a three-week programme of classical music, theatre, opera and dance, or the festival of modern music at Glastonbury. They will probably have seen news items about film festivals. Ask the children if their parents have been to such a festival and what it was like.

Religious festivals abound in all religions. Ask the children to tell you of the ones they already know and to draw a picture of one of them. Explore various other festivals using books in your library. Ask parents of children from other countries to come and talk about festivals in their country.

I like Hanukkah. It has eight nights and we light an extra candle every night. We have good things to eat.

One of the most famous festivals is in New Orleans in March every year called the Mardi Gras. People dress up in wonderful costumes and play jazz music as they process through the streets with lorries pulling floats with a 'King and Queen' leading the parade. People throw trinkets called 'throws' to the crowd. (See http://www.neworleansonline.com/neworleans/mardigras.)

You could organise a festival in your classroom – it could be a spring or summer festival to celebrate the end of a term's work.

If you want to organise a children's party, Mardi Gras style, this website will help: http://www.mardigrasday.com/mardigras/party.php.

Exploring various cultures – older children

Festivals

Explain that all our family parties for weddings and other celebrations are festivals or feast days. Talk about these with the children and about how they feel at them. Most countries around the world have festivals when people dress up and parade, have feasts and parties.

In Valencia in Spain, people spend a whole year making and painting large sculptures called *ninots* from paper-mâché, wood and wax. Some are funny, others are serious. Then on the final night of their festival on 19th March, St Joseph's Day, one *ninot* is chosen to be saved while all the rest, often as many as 300 of them, are burned in a festival of fireworks and fire.

In China, the Eve of the Chinese New Year is a time when as many Chinese people as possible try to get home for reunion dinners with their families. This festival is in different spring months each year and lasts for 15 days, ending with the Lantern Festival on the evening of the fifteenth day. During the Lantern Festival, children go out at night carrying bright lanterns. In ancient times, the lanterns were fairly simple, for only the Emperor and noblemen had large ornate ones; in modern times, lanterns can be decorated with many designs and are sometimes in shapes of animals. People without lanterns enjoy watching the many lantern parades.

If you want to organise a Chinese New Year party for your children, visit

http://www.kidspartyfun.com/pages/themes/chinesenewyear.html.

Use your world map or globe and ask the children to work in small groups to find out about other festivals around the world. Ask each group to describe the festival, draw people partaking and write down some of the special party foods the people will be enjoying. Unite the children's work in a book or make a display of festivals around the world.

Learning at home (ask children to choose one or two)

1. Ask children who have been to festivals themselves to draw pictures and write words to describe what happened, how it looked and how they felt.
2. Ask other children to talk to their parents and families about festivals that they have been to and to draw and write about these occasions.

Exploring various cultures – younger children

Music

In Circle Time, talk to the children about the kinds of music you have in school; about their singing and listening to music. Ask the children to think of their favourite school and home songs and to finish the sentence:

I like to play the tambourine best.

'I like to sing ...'

Examine your school musical instruments and ask the children to think of the different sounds they make and how these sounds are made. Ask them which they like to play and to finish the sentence:

'I like to play the ... best.'

Music affects our feelings and can make us feel joyful or sad. Ask them to tell you how they feel when they listen to or play different kinds of music.

Explain that children in different countries also like to listen to and make music and that their music may be very different to the kinds of music that we normally listen to. If you can, obtain music tapes or CDs of songs and music from other cultures for the children to listen to; talk about the different kinds of sounds that make that music and how these sounds are made.

Look again at your school instruments and talk about how these instruments are made. Can the children see that people could make instruments similar to these using odd pieces of wood or metal and that anything that can make a noise can be incorporated into an orchestra or band? Explain that many of the musical instruments in developing cultures are 'home-made' in so far as they are made from whatever is at hand. They may be tuned instruments or percussion. Can you help them to make a musical instrument from junk?

Talk about the occasions when we use music, for example, celebrations, festivals, marching bands, orchestral concerts, opera. Help the children to understand that music is a very real part of all cultures and that music is something we can share even if we cannot understand the language of people from other countries.

Exploring various cultures – older children

Music

Talk about the music we know and love in this country. Ask the children to help you to list the various kinds of music that we listen to and show how diverse it can be, for example, jazz, pipe bands, orchestral music, opera. Talk about the Eurovision Song Contest and how European countries compete to win the award for the best song. Why are so many songs in English?

Talk about how musical instruments are made, and how our sophisticated instruments today have evolved from simple home-made instruments of our ancestors. Talk about different families of instruments, percussion, woodwind, strings, brass and keyboard and how they are arranged in an orchestra.

Explain that many other cultures have a proud tradition of music and often their instruments are made from whatever they can find from where they live. Ask the children to think of music from other cultures, for example, steel bands, Australian didgeridoo music, Italian operatic music, Spanish flamenco music, African drum music, Indian sitar music. Use CDs of music from various cultures to help the children to understand the universal appeal of music which we can share and which crosses the boundaries of language.

Explain that in many cultures the sounds in the music have evolved from the instruments they have made and the instruments have been made by using whatever materials were at hand.

Ask the children to work in groups and to choose a different country from your world map. Ask them to investigate the music from that country, using search engines on the Internet, encyclopedias (including Encarta) and books from your library. Build up a display about the music from these countries.

Learning at home

Ask each child to make a musical instrument from various materials that they will have at home, e.g. wood, metal, skin, earthenware or glass, and to bring their instrument to school to share with the class. If possible encourage them to organise small group bands and use their instruments to play a tune for your class to enjoy. They will need time and space to practise.

Read the story to the children and then carry out the activities below.

Paloma and the Moors and Christians

Paloma was seven years old and lived in Spain. She was very excited because it was almost time for the festival of the Moors and Christians. Paloma lived in a little town in the province of Valencia in Spain with her parents and her two little sisters. The family owned and ran the little bakery in the town and Paloma was often awake early in the morning because her father had to get up early to get the bread started and light the ovens. Her mother stayed in bed until it was time to wake Paloma, give her breakfast and get ready for school. On this morning, though, Paloma was wide awake and got up straight away before her mother had even woken.

Paloma looked out of the window. Winter was nearly over but it was not daylight because the sun was not up yet. With the help of the street lights she could see the decorations in the main street. There were streamers and flags right across the road from house to house in the narrow street. Strings of coloured lights swayed gently in the early morning breeze.

She heard the sounds of men's voices and of metal being moved. Opening the window, she leaned out and could see men putting up strong metal barriers alongside the kerbs of the pavements. They did this so that people would be safe from the floats and horses in the procession later that day. Soon lorries would come to bring lots of folding chairs and men would set them out all along the route for the people watching to sit on. Then everything would be ready for the celebrations that night!

All the shops would be closed except theirs, for people had to buy bread and cakes every day, but they would close very early so that people could get ready for the procession. Even the small supermarket would be closed on this special day. Paloma smiled to herself, she could hardly wait. She remembered the processions from other years; the noise, the music, the excitement. She turned away from the window and closed it before turning to look at her dress. It was nearly all white with blue lace and ribbons on it. She had tried it on several times and felt really beautiful in it. Today she wouldn't need to wear her glasses because she was going to sit in the float with all the children from the houses around where she lived. Her parents and two little sisters would sit on the chairs, watching. There would be 15 floats from different areas of the town and they would process through the streets, up and down, ending up at the little church that looked down on the pretty white town.

Every year the grown-ups in the town had lots of meetings about the Moors and Christians festival. She knew it was something to do with the history of the area, when the Moors who had conquered the Spanish were defeated by the Christians. Each year they chose the most important people for the procession; the most important was the chief of the Moors and he would process first in front of all his men. Then would come the Christians and they would be dressed up in glittering finery. Most people didn't think of the history of the Moors and Christians – only of the pageant, the dressing up, the procession and the feasting.

The two main parts to the procession were separated; first the Moors with the chief sitting on a huge chair, surrounded by his important soldiers on a float, made on a lorry; this would be followed by their foot soldiers. They would march, in time, very slowly as they moved along the processional route. Then would come the horses; fine Spanish horses ridden by experts who would make the horses rear and gallop as they rode up and down between the two sections of the procession. The Christians would be next; their chiefs sitting in their finery followed by their foot soldiers also marching slowly in time with the loud and energetic music. There would be bands; at least three this year; one at the beginning, one in the middle and one at the end. And after them all would be the children on their floats, all dressed up in their finery.

It was a very special day for Paloma. For the first time she would be sitting on one of the floats, right at the end of the procession along with other children she knew. They would be paraded through the little town, throwing sweets to the children and grown-ups watching. In other years she had been one of the little ones watching and trying to catch the sweets. Today would be a day to remember. Her first procession!

Activities

Make a list of all the feelings that Paloma would have had on the day of the festival, from getting up in the morning, getting ready, being in the parade and later when it was all over.

Think about what Paloma would have said to you if she had met you the next day. Write what she would have said about the festival.

Imagine that your school is going to have a new festival or procession. What will it be about? Write a description of it, saying how it would be organised, what you would do, how you would be dressed; the feelings of the people taking part and the feelings of those watching.

Think of a procession that you have seen and draw a picture of it. Was there music? How did the music affect everybody? What kinds of instruments were played and who played them? Were there people dancing? What did they look like? What kinds of clothes did they wear? Were there any animals? Was there a feast at the end?

Think of a special celebration or occasion that you have attended at your school, perhaps a fun day, fund-raising day, sports day or end of term concert. Were you a part of it or did you just watch it? Draw a picture about this and write why you think it was an important occasion. Write how the people organising the occasion planned it and how they felt as they were planning, rehearsing and trying to get everything right. Did you play a part? Write about it if you did. Write about how everyone felt when it was all over.

Exploring various cultures – Reflection

In Circle Time, initiate a general discussion about what children now know about the lives of people in various cultures. Ask the children to look through their Global Citizenship folders and read the work there. Ask them to add to their list of the children they have worked with. Who has worked with the most children? What do they remember most about each of the sections?

Talk about how they feel about people who have come from other countries to live here and the benefits we gain from so much rich, diverse culture.

Talk about games and toys that children use in different parts of the world. Were they surprised to find that so many of their old-fashioned toys and games are universal? Remind them about the foods they found out about and how different foods have been brought to the UK from different parts of the world.

Remind them that we may appear to be wealthy in terms of what we have but that children in developing countries may be just as wealthy in terms of family life and love from their extended families who may have to work hard together to find a good way to live.

Ask the children to use the activity sheet 'Other countries' to record some of the things they now know about people's lives in other countries.

Getting involved

Talk about their part in respecting the ways of people from different countries and of understanding and accepting the various lifestyles that these people lead. Remind them that as part of a global community we must recognise the values of people from all countries and accept them into our community.

Global challenges

Remind the children that not all people in this country are fair to those who come to live here. If they, as children, can promote a positive attitude towards people from different cultures, things will get better. It is only by everyone being fair to, and having empathy for, people from other cultures that our world will become a better and fairer place. They are the future; it's in their hands.

Harrig

A visitor named Harrig has come to your school from planet Zigor.

Draw Harrig in the circle and write in the boxes.

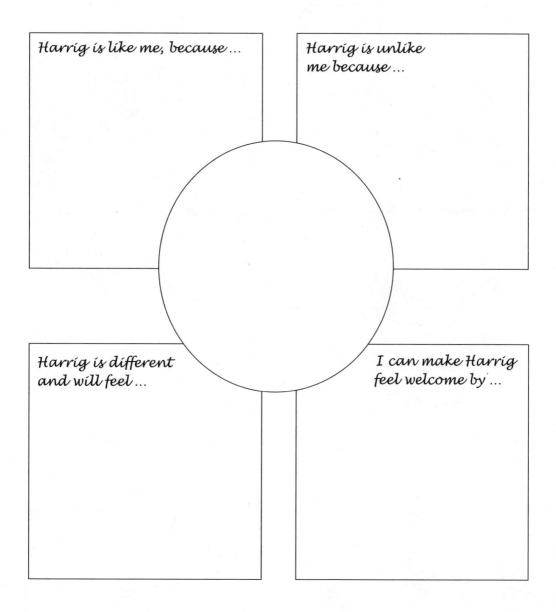

Harrig is like me, because ...

Harrig is unlike me because ...

Harrig is different and will feel ...

I can make Harrig feel welcome by ...

On the other side of the paper write a story about Harrig.

A new game

Work in pairs to design a card game or a board game about life in a different country. Draw the game. On the other side, write what children in another country could use to make and play the game, how to play it and the rules.

Other countries

Think of all the things you now know about people who live in other countries and fill in each box with a drawing. Write about each thing on the other side of the paper.

Draw a food from another country.	Draw a fruit or vegetable from another country.
Draw a costume or dress worn by people in another country.	Draw a festival from another country.
Draw something about music from another country.	Draw children playing with a toy or game in another country.

Section 5

Democracy

Focus

This section will help children to understand how a democratic way of life will help all people to become valued citizens of the world. In particular the children will be exploring the notions of:

- what is democracy?
- free speech
- moral issues
- media impact
- currency and resources
- fair trade
- voting
- political issues
- security.

Remind the children to keep their Global Citizenship folders up to date by putting into them any work they do in this section and to keep a record of the children they work with.

Look at the activity sheets; 'Rights and responsibilities', 'Democratic or not?', 'A personal budget plan' and 'My Manifesto' at the end of the section to see if they are appropriate for your children.

Democracy – younger children

What is democracy?

Explain to the children what democracy is. Help them to understand that it means a kind of fairness; a democratic country is one where the people themselves choose their government, set the rules and try to abide by them. In a democracy, people should have a lot of freedom and life is fair for everyone.

I would like to change the rule about playing in the home corner. I think 5 would be better than 4.

Talk about your classroom. Do you run it in a democratic way? Ask the children to tell you whether they feel equal and if the rules are fair for all. Who made the rules? Did you give them an opportunity to play their part in this?

Remind them about the work they did about rules in the 'Fairness' section of this book. Ask them to think about the rules in your classroom and if they would like to change any or add to them. Explain to them that rulers of countries look at the existing rules and that, as things change, they may change rules to make things better.

Talk about the rights and responsibilities that the children have in your classroom. Can they help you to make a list of their rights? For example, they have the right to learn, to play, to be helped, to be treated fairly by you and other children. Use the activity sheet 'Rights and responsibilities' at the end of this section.

Talk about the responsibilities of the children in your classroom. What do you expect from them, for example, to listen, to pay attention, to work quietly and not disturb others. Ask them to help you to make a list of their responsibilities. Do these look a bit like your classroom rules?

Ask the children to talk to their families about how their home is run – is it run democratically? Ask them to think about who makes the decisions and why.

Remind the children that in a democratic society people have the right to be treated fairly and equally. Explain that many countries are not governed democratically and that people who live there are often not treated fairly.

Democracy – older children

What is democracy?

Ask the children to complete the activity sheet 'Democratic or not?'.

The word 'democracy' comes from the Greek, (*demos*, 'the people'; *kratein*, 'to rule'). It is a political system in which the people of a country rule through any form of government they choose to establish. The officials in a democracy should directly reflect the known or ascertained views of their constituents, sometimes subordinating their own judgement. Explain that modern democracy includes individual freedom, which entitles citizens to the choice and responsibility of shaping their own careers and conducting their own affairs; it means that we are all equal before the law; adults are all allowed to vote for government and everyone is entitled to education and health care.

Such features have been proclaimed in great historic documents, for example, the US Declaration of Independence, which asserted the right to life, liberty, and the pursuit of happiness; the French Declaration of the Rights of Man and of the Citizen, which affirmed the principles of civil liberty and of equality before the law; and the Atlantic Charter.

Talk to the children about democracy and what it means in your school. Who makes the rules? Is there a school council? If you have a school council or have other ways in which children represent their class, talk about how these people were chosen, what they do and how they make sure that things are fair for everyone.

Ask the children to work in pairs to find out about the democratic system in your local area. Your local council would help; perhaps you could invite someone into school to explain how the system works, how the people in power were elected and what they do.

Learning at home

Ask the children to find out how other countries are governed and when, if ever, they became democratic countries. Ask them to make a list of which countries are run democratically and which are not. They can use books, encyclopedias and the Internet. Back in school, amalgamate these lists to make one.

Democracy – younger children

Free speech

Ask the children to think about what the phrase 'free speech' might mean. Does it mean that we can all say just anything? Has what we say got to be true? Can we say true things that will hurt people's feelings?

Talk about the words we use; those that are kind and those that can be hurtful. Ask the children to tell you some kind words so that you can make a list.

Explain that using these words makes everyone feel good. Ask the children to think about how they use their voices when they are talking to people. Can they say something that sounds kind in a kind voice and the same thing in an unkind voice? Help them to understand that the voice they use and their body language are just as important as the words they use. Use drama to play about with these ideas.

Talk about people who don't always tell the truth. Ask them how they feel when someone tells them a lie. Can they ever believe anything that this person says? How do they feel when someone says something unkind about them or their family? Ask them to draw this.

Ask the children to think about a person they know who is different in some way from other people, perhaps they are not very clever or have some kind of illness. Ask them to think about how that person would feel if people said unkind words about their difference.

Ask the children to think about their religion and about someone they know who has a different religion. How would they feel if this person said unkind things about their religion? Ask them to do the same thing about colour of skin and race.

Explain that in this country it is safe to say what we feel as long as it is true but in some countries people may not feel safe to talk against the government or various religions.

Democracy – older children

Free speech

Talk about the issues raised on the opposite page for younger children and organise a debate with opposing sides:

'Free speech is always OK.'
'Free speech is not always OK.'

After the debate ask the children to work in small groups to make two lists, one of situations when free speech is OK and one when it is not. Come together as a class and share the lists. Are they all acceptable? Can you amalgamate all the lists into two?

Ask the children to help you to make a list about the kinds of things that we must be careful not to say to others, for example, bullying words, hurtful words, words about race or colour. Talk to the children about why they have suggested their words for your list.

Discuss the consequences for people if they ignore these conventions and are too outspoken about the things on your list. Will what they say just hurt people's feelings or will there be more worrying consequences?

Remind the children about the need to be truthful; you might like to talk about the story of the boy who cried 'wolf'. Explain that lies can have worrying consequences, especially if a small lie grows and spreads like ripples in a pond.

Ask the children to find out what 'slanderous' and 'libellous' mean. Discuss the possible consequences when people use words in either of these ways.

Explain that freedom of speech or freedom of expression, both oral and written, are always desirable except in cases where justification for restriction is given, as in cases of libel or national security.

Learning at home

Ask the children, with help from their families, to write a page about the wartime directive 'Careless talk costs lives'.

Democracy – younger children

Moral issues

Talk to the children about the qualities that we would like people in all countries to have so that our world would be a better place, for example, honesty, truthfulness, goodness, fairness. These qualities are difficult for young children to understand and are best illustrated through the following stories:

Honesty

In Mrs Brown's class children always put their paintings on a rack to dry. One day James put his wet painting there and it touched another one, leaving a long black mark all along that painting. James didn't know what to do. When the children collected their paintings to take home, Sara was really upset to see that her painting was spoiled. She told Mrs Brown who asked the children if they knew anything about it. No one said anything. James looked at the floor. He didn't know what to do; he didn't want to get into trouble.

I think James should say sorry to Sara.

Ask the children what they think about James's behaviour. Was it good? Was it honest? Ask the children what they would say to James about what he did and what he didn't do. Ask them to tell you what they think James could do next to make it better. Make a list of their suggestions and then ask them to choose one of them to draw.

Stealing

The children in Mrs Brown's class were not supposed to take toys to school. But when it was their birthday, they could take just one toy to show. On Azif's birthday he took a set of small Lego people to school to show everyone. Afterwards they were put on the shelf so that they were safe but when it was time to go home, one of the little people was missing. Azif was really upset. The teacher was cross and asked who had taken the little man. No one answered, but Rachel felt in her pocket and fingered the little man. She didn't know what to do. The teacher said that this was stealing and when she asked everyone if they knew where it was, Rachel said 'no'.

Talk with the children about what Rachel could do. Stress the importance of honesty and truthfulness in our everyday lives. Explain that good citizenship is all about people being truthful, honest and having good morals.

Democracy – older children

Moral issues

Discuss the two scenarios on the opposite page and ask the children to tell you what they think about the morals of James and Rachel. Help them to realise that young children often lie because they are afraid they will get into trouble; they need guidance and understanding to learn good moral values.

Talk about the importance of children of their age being truthful and honest. Ask the children to think of incidences in their lives when they have been tempted to be dishonest or untruthful. Are any of them willing to talk about these occasions and what they did?

Ask the children to think of a story they have read where one of the characters was dishonest or untruthful. Ask them to write a description of the character and say what she or he did that was wrong. Ask them to think up and write down a new action for the character to do so that they are not dishonest or untruthful. This will, undoubtedly, spoil the original storyline.

Bring into the classroom some local and national newspapers. Ask the children to work in pairs to find reports of people who have done something to hurt or harm another person, for example, stealing from them, burgling them, fighting them. Ask them to describe the incident as though they were the innocent victim of the action. Ask them to write down their feelings about the incident.

Explain to the children that official organisations are not always morally upright and that, though we think our government may be honest and true, there are governments in other parts of the world that are corrupt and morally dangerous. Discuss the effects on the people when a government does not rule its country in a morally upright way.

Learning at home

Ask the children to talk to their families about issues where people in our or other countries seem to have been morally corrupt. What kinds of things occurred for people to think this? What were the effects of these people's wrong-doing? Discuss these issues back in school.

Democracy – younger children

Media impact

Ask the children to tell you what kinds of things they see advertised on TV.

Collect their responses and make a chart of the kinds of things that they remember, under headings such as foods, drinks, toys.

Talk about whether they think that all the things they see advertised on TV are really true. Ask whether they think that the advertisers are really honest about some of the things they say about, for instance, breakfast cereals. Do they think that if they eat the cereal, they will be able to do the things that the advertisers suggest?

Ask the children to close their eyes and think of a TV advert that they know. Ask them to open their eyes and remember the picture in their heads. Ask them to draw a picture of what the TV is advertising and to write whether they think it is a good advert or not and whether they would like to buy the product.

I think this TV advert is trying to make you buy the toy.

Share these pictures and writing in Circle Time and talk about adverts which are really important to know about and which are just people trying to persuade parents to buy things for their children.

Ask the children, when they watch TV that night to look carefully at the advertising and try to think which are good and important things for us to know and which are just persuaders. The next day, discuss what they think.

Talk about newspapers and the kinds of advertising they see there. Do the children think that these things are always true or do some adverts make the product look better than it really is? Talk about why this could be.

Talk about the news they see on TV. What do the children think about the news? Is it always true? Do they think that people try to make things sound greater than they really are? Remind the children to think carefully before they believe everything they see on TV or in the papers.

Democracy – older children

Media impact

Use the ideas from the facing page to provide a starting point for this work.

Talk about how powerfully TV can change images to make them look true when we know that what we are seeing is impossible, for example Superman flying, or aliens doing supposedly magical things. Ask the children to give you examples of the impossibility of some of the things they see on TV and talk about these.

Explain that while this is usually part of the magic of film and TV, there is a different side to these magical tricks and that sometimes advertisers promise things that are not true. Ask the children to give examples of the kinds of tricks advertisers use to make children persuade their parents to buy things, for example by enclosing cards, games, tokens or toys in with a product.

Explain that the whole purpose of advertising is to persuade us to buy the products and that we need to be aware of this and resist temptation which might make us buy things that are unsuitable or unnecessary.

Talk about the programmes that some of them may see on TV that encourage older people to buy things directly from the TV, things that they haven't had the opportunity to see or touch to make sure they are good quality. Talk about TV programmes that try to persuade people to gamble money. Can they see that this is a way for the advertisers to get money?

Bring into school some current newspaper headlines that have sensationalised an event so that people will buy the papers. Talk about the ethics of these tactics and explain that sometimes things are printed which are not strictly true.

Learning at home

Ask the children to look carefully at what they see on TV, or in newspapers or magazines and to list examples of advertising that is aimed at very young children to try to persuade them to get parents to buy the product. Ask them to bring their list to school to share with the class. Use these to make a chart of good, not so good or bad advertising tactics; add warnings in speech bubbles.

Democracy – younger children

Currency and resources

Ask the children to put up a thumb if they get pocket money. Count how many. Ask them to raise a little finger if they have to do anything to get their money. Ask volunteers to say what they do.

Talk about pocket money and how the children spend it. Do they sometimes save up for something that costs a lot? Do they sometimes ask someone in their family to lend them more money to buy what they want? Talk about lending and borrowing money and explain that banks charge people who want to do this. Explain that when grown-ups want to buy a house or a car they usually pay a part of the money when they get the car or house and then arrange to pay the rest over some years. Explain that banks and other organisations charge a lot for this and that sometimes the people pay twice as much for a house by the time they have paid it all.

Explain to the children that money is a reward for work done and that all countries have some kind of currency. Talk about how people managed in the past when there was no money and they had to barter or 'swap' things to get things that they wanted.

Ask the children to think of something that they want and something that they already have that they would swap for it. Ask them to draw a picture about this and to use a speech bubble to say what the things are.

Tell the children that countries are rich or poor according to how much money they have and that . this money could be in gold or other valuable metals or oil. Explain that this money is a resource that will buy things, such as food or equipment for the people of that country.

Talk about other resources that a country has, such as crops they grow, minerals they can mine and skills of the people that can be used to help other nations. Ask the children to draw a picture of people in their family showing the skills they have and to label these skills, for example, 'daddy can cook'.

Democracy – older children

Currency and resources

Ask the children to tell you what they know about the monetary system in this country. Do they understand about interest paid on savings and interest that you pay on borrowings? Ask the children to tell you what they do when they have more money than they need immediately (spare money) and also when they don't have enough to buy something they need or want. Ask them to make a written record of this on a folded paper; on one half, write about what they do with spare money and on the other, what they do when they need money. Discuss this. Talk about budgets and how to organise finances. Show them how to keep an account of their money with double pages, one for income and the other for expenditure. Use the 'A personal budget plan' activity sheet.

Explain that the government of this country has no money of its own; the money they use is money that has been taken from the people in taxes. They have to have a budget and use the money wisely. Ask the children to tell you what the government spends money on and make a list, for example, health care, education, buildings. Tell the children that it is the same in local government; they have to budget and balance their accounts of money received from council tax and money spent on local amenities.

Ask the children to work in pairs and make a list of other resources that we have and have had in the UK, under four headings; things dug from the ground, things grown in the ground, manufactured products, and skills. Collect and discuss their ideas and add to them if necessary.

Explain that all countries have natural resources which should be used for the good of that country but that in some countries these are in the hands of a few people who may use the natural wealth they generate for themselves.

Learning at home

Ask the children to investigate currencies and natural resources of a country of their choice. Amalgamate their findings at school and make lists under each country. Which countries are rich in resources and which are poor?

Democracy – younger children

Fairtrade

Ask the children to tell you which foods and goods come from this country and make a list, such as apples, potatoes, clothes, toys. Explain that in this country, the people who grow or make these goods are paid a fair wage and do their work in good conditions because the government has set up a minimum wage for everyone. Tell them that in other countries this is not always the case.

Explain that in some developing countries children have to do quite a lot of the unskilled work that is necessary to produce goods. This is often because their parents need the little money that they earn. The people who employ them like children to work because they don't have to pay them much. It means that the children do not have time to go to school to learn and so may not be able to get good jobs themselves when they are grown up.

Tell them that very young children used to have to work in this country many years ago. Tell or remind them of the story of Tom in *The Water Babies* and explain that children were useful because they could do many things as they were small. In factories, young children would run between machines to pick up bobbins or waste; on farms they could pick produce. Nowadays, there are laws in this country to prevent young children from working, and laws to make sure that children go to school to get an education.

Ask the children if they have ever seen this logo before.

Tell them that it is called the FAIRTRADE Mark and is put on foods that have been properly grown and sold at a fair price to supermarkets so that the people who grow the food get a fair price for growing it. Ask the children to look through their family's food cupboard to see if they can find anything with this Mark. If they can, ask them to bring the container to school when it is empty.

Put a picture of the Fairtrade logo on your whiteboard or screen so that the children can see it. Ask the children to draw a picture of themselves buying some chocolate with this logo on it and to write a sentence about why it is called 'Fairtrade' chocolate. Ask them to draw a large picture of the logo on the back of their paper and to take this work home for their parents to see.

Democracy – older children

Fairtrade

(Visit www.papapaa.org. for teaching resources about Fair trade.)

Ask the children to discuss the following:

> When you go shopping, what is your main concern? Is it how the thing looks? Is it that it is a cheap price? Do you ever think of the price being fair to the original grower or maker? Is it important to you that people get a fair deal?

Talk about the people who support Fairtrade products. Do they know that in many countries the people who grow or make things only get a very small part of what we pay when we buy them in this country? Explain that in some countries suppliers are not paid enough money for their goods to live a fair life and that many are very poor. For example, a cocoa farmer in Ghana (in 2006) would only get one per cent of the selling price of a chocolate bar. Some children can't go to school because they have to work for their parents or because their parents can't pay for schooling. With Fairtrade it is hoped that things are changing.

In some countries the government has allowed cheap imports of foods such as rice. The people who grow this food cannot sell it for a fair price because shoppers buy the cheaper food. This means that the growers in their country do not earn enough money to have a fair standard of life. In some countries the growers and manufacturers have formed themselves into co-operatives to try to obtain a fair price for their goods. Where this is working, the people are now able to live a better life and educate their children.

Ask the children to find out from the Internet as much as they can about the Fairtrade movement and the World Trade Organisation (WTO). If they put 'Fairtrade' into their search engine they will find out a lot about the people who support Fairtrade and the ways in which this helps countries to develop.

Learning at home

Give the children a copy of the Fairtrade logo known as the FAIRTRADE Mark on the facing page. Ask them to look around shops and list the foods they can buy that have this Mark. Ask them to talk to their families about Fairtrade foods and why they buy them or not. Ask each child to write a page about some of the Fairtrade foods and what they think happens in the country of origin when people buy them.

Democracy – younger children

Voting

Talk to the children about how groups can make choices. In children's games they often draw straws or 'dip' to choose a leader or starter for a game. Can they tell you some of the 'dips' they use? Explain that this is 'chance'.

Talk to the children about how we in this country choose our government. Explain the system of a secret ballot and how this is necessary so that people will feel free to vote the way they want; not as other people want to make them.

Do the children vote in your class? If so talk about the way you do it. Talk about the difference between the 'hands up if …' kind of voting and a secret ballot. Do the children in your class think they would vote differently if you always used a secret ballot?

Ask the children to draw a picture of themselves voting the way they think is most fair. Help them to complete a speech bubble about their voting.

Ask the children how they would feel if you would only allow certain children or just boys in your class to vote. Is that fair?

Tell the children that many years ago not all people could vote for their government representatives; once, only very important men had a vote. Later all male citizens were allowed to vote, but some people 'bought' their votes or bribed them to vote a certain way. Women were not allowed to vote in the UK until 1918, after women had disrupted society to make men allow them to vote.

Ask the children if they know what kinds of things are decided by voting outside school. Talk about how people vote in local elections and national elections. Hold an election for some position in your class and ask volunteers to put themselves up for election by standing up and telling everyone how well they would carry out that job. Give the candidates time to prepare a 'speech' and ask children to vote. Hold a secret ballot to ensure fairness.

Democracy – older children

Voting

Talk about voting as a fair way of making a choice. Explain that in the UK we choose our local and central governments by voting for candidates.

Explain that political candidates write a manifesto to say what they will do or not do if they are elected into local or national government. Emphasise that a manifesto is a way of advertising; sometimes people put things in their manifesto which they can't do. Ask the children to think of the kinds of things they would like a local candidate to say they would do. Ask them to make a list of the things that would be good for your locality. Ask them to work in groups to write a manifesto for an imaginary candidate using some of the ideas. Discuss this and vote by ballot for the best candidate. Discuss the result.

Ask the children to help you to choose someone to represent your class on a local TV programme. Explain that this is not a popularity competition and that they should choose a leader for certain qualities. Ask them to work in pairs to make a list of the qualities this person should have in order to represent your school. Ask each pair to merge with another pair to amalgamate the lists. Repeat this doubling up until you have one class list and display this.

Now ask all the children in your class to write a manifesto to try to persuade everyone in the class to vote for them to be the representative. Use the manifesto template at the end of this section. Display these manifestos and ask the children to vote for four. Ask these four children to give a speech about why they think they should be the representative before asking all the class to vote for their choice.

Explain that in a few countries not all people are allowed to vote; in some, women still do not have a vote. Literacy is often a qualification. In many countries people who have been convicted of a serious crime are deprived of voting rights.

Learning at home

Using your world map, ask children to choose a country and ask them to investigate the democratic process there. They can ask their families as well as using books and the Internet. At school, share and discuss their findings.

Democracy – younger children

Political issues

Remind the children about voting. Tell them that in this country there are three main political parties and other smaller parties. Make a list of these. Tell the children some of the current issues that these parties want to address, for example the 'Green' party wants to protect the environment. Do they know the names of the principal people in government? Talk about them and their jobs.

Show pictures of the Houses of Parliament in London. Tell them of the two houses; the House of Commons and the House of Lords; that the word 'parliament' comes from the French *parler* which means to talk. The European parliament is in Brussels and Strasbourg, with members from all the EC countries.

Explain that people vote for the person they want to be their member of parliament (MP) in the House of Commons, in England; each MP works for the people in their own constituency and they also go to London to help to run the country. Scotland, Wales and Northern Ireland have their own parliaments.

> Mrs Jones our councillor came to see us.

Many years ago only rich and important people could be a member of parliament; nowadays anyone can try to become an MP by telling people what they will do for their constituency and the country and getting people to vote for them. A prospective MP has to tell the people what he or she will do for the constituency. Remind the children of the work they did in the 'voting' section when some of them spoke about what they would do if they were elected for a position in your class. Explain that an MP has to have this written down and it is called a 'manifesto'. Candidates make sure that all the people in their constituency have a copy of this. They hold meetings and ask people to come and hear them speak about what they would do if they were elected as MP and finally there is an election.

Invite your local MP or councillor to come into school to talk to the children about their work. Ask the children to write the invitation and make sure that they have thought out some questions they want to ask. Write these questions on your board for your visitor to see. Make sure that children write to thank their visitor.

Democracy – older children

Political issues

Find out what the children know about local government in this country. Do they know the name of the local fiscal area where your school is, the names of the people who run your local government and their political party?

Write down the names of the three or more parties that are represented in your local area and divide the class into three or more main groups, each to investigate a different party's promises. Make sure they know the area of the constituency where your school is, the party in power and the name of the leader of the council. Ask them to find out what councillors actually do; their roles and responsibilities; how money is raised; who decides on the budget and how it is spent. Your local councillors may be willing to help you. Ask the children to write up their group's findings to share with the class.

Talk about the government, the various political parties and what they stand for; is this always the case? Do some MPs have other roles as well as that of caring for their constituency? Explain about the Cabinet and that MPs divide their time between their local area and their office in parliament.

Discuss with the children issues such as the current government of this country, the party in power, the Cabinet, the principal members of the Cabinet and their roles; how the Commons is organised and who is in charge there. Perhaps you could watch a parliamentary session on TV.

Using your world map, ask children to select a country and investigate the political situation there. Does their chosen country have a stable government? Is it a democratic country? Do the people in power there do the best for their people or is there unrest? Share this work in the classroom and ask the children to reflect on the benefits of living in a democratic country.

Learning at home

Ask the children to find out about how British parliaments first came into being, answering such questions as: Who ruled the country before? When was the first parliament? Who was the first British Prime Minister? Why was a parliament created? What is Black Rod? What is the monarch's role?

Democracy – younger children

Security

Talk to the children about who keeps our community safe. Do you know your local police or schools liaison officer? If so, ask the children to write a letter to ask him/her to come into school to talk about what they do to keep your locality safe. Are there other people such as locality wardens who help? Ask the children to help you to compile a list of the things that all these people do in your local area to make sure the community is safe for everyone.

Ask the children to draw a picture of a police officer and to write about what they do.

Talk with the children about other areas of the police service, such as detectives who solve crime, officers who go to court to give evidence to convict criminals and those who go out on the streets during demonstrations to keep law and order.

This is PC Kazim. She keeps us safe.

Explain about the people chosen to judge people who have been arrested for some crime and the different kinds of courts to deal with different offences. Explain that a magistrate is someone who runs a local court and deals with less serious offences; a judge presides over a crown court.

Tell them about Toad in *The Wind in the Willows* who had to go to court because he was a bad driver. Ask the children to think of any other stories they know where people have done wrong and had to go to court.

Explain that punishment for doing wrong is meant to match the crime. When people do very bad things, their punishment is more severe than when they do things that are not quite so bad. They may have to work in the community or they may pay a fine or go to prison.

Ask them to think of something a child might do wrong and a suitable punishment for that. Ask them to draw this. Is the punishment fair?

Democracy – older children

Security

Ask the children to think about who or what makes this country secure. Make a list of what they offer and discuss each idea. Did they mention the police? The army? The secret service? CCTV? Discuss all these.

Remind them that they have a responsibility to keep themselves safe. Discuss how we do this at home and school and what to do if our safety is threatened.

Discuss national security and whose job that is. The government's Home Office at present is the department that deals with this. Ask the children to log on to the Home Office website and find out about local and national issues. Ask them to find answers to the following questions:

How should people deal with local acts of unsocial behaviour?

What should grown-ups do if they see a crime is being committed?

Who should they themselves contact if they think a crime is being planned?

What should someone their age do if they see a crime being committed?

Ask the children to discuss the following:

'The main role of the police service is to conduct local, intelligence-based patrols and to take part in crime prevention initiatives, often targeted at specific problem areas.'

Learning at home

Ask the children to think of what they need to keep safe from. Ask them to suggest appropriate agencies that are there to take care of our safety and security in various places or from dangers. Ask each child to make a chart similar to the one below, adding other places and writing alongside whose job it is to keep them safe and secure. The first one has been done for them ...

places/dangers	whose job is it?
fire	Ours, by having a sensible family escape route. The Fire Service.
water	
trains	

Lucia's story

Lucia lives in the Ashanti region of Ghana. She is grown up now, but when she was a little girl she lived with her parents who had a very small farm where they grew cacao trees. When her father planted the trees they were very small but they grew quickly in the hot weather and soon the trees looked very tall to her. The family grew the trees to get the cocoa beans or seeds from the trees. When she was a little girl she helped her parents with the cocoa harvest. The beans had to be picked by hand and Lucia, even when she was very small, would help to spread them out in the sunshine so that they would dry before they were sold. Her parents would sell the cocoa beans to manufacturing companies to be sent by ship to Rotterdam in Holland where they were made into cocoa powder or chocolate. They did not get very much money for the beans in spite of all their hard work. They had to make the little money they got from the harvest last for a whole year for everything, for food, clothes and medicines. There would be no more money until the next harvest.

Lucia didn't have many things. Her few clothes were usually made from other people's old clothes that her mother cut down and sewed to fit her. Their food was just the kinds of vegetables and fruit that they could grow on a little part of the farm, so you can see that it was a very poor life really. In spite of this, Lucia was a happy little girl who was greatly loved by her parents and friends.

When Lucia was old enough, she went to school every day with her friends and enjoyed learning. When she was older, part of her studies were about the vegetation in Ghana and that's how she learned all about the cacao tree. She learned about the growing of the trees, about the diseases that could spoil the crop, the harvesting of the fruit seeds or beans and how they were fermented to give them their distinctive flavour.

When she left school, she wanted to work with her parents on the farm but they said there was not enough money from the cocoa beans so she had to find another job, working in a shop. What Lucia didn't know was that sometimes the people her parents sold the beans to would cheat them over the weight of the beans. They also paid them very little, only just enough money for her parents to live a very poor life; sometimes they got almost nothing at all. That meant they had no money for food or clothes. The people who bought the beans and packed them to go on board the large ships to Europe got a lot of money from them and were quite wealthy people.

Then, in 1993, everything changed. The cocoa farmers got together and formed a fair trade co-operative. This meant that all the farms were owned and managed by the farmers themselves. Together they made sure that accurate weighing scales were used; they organised the sale of all their cocoa beans and got a much fairer price. All the small-scale cocoa farmers now had a much better life and Lucia was able to leave her job and go to work on the farm.

A few years later, a project organised by a charity sent people to Ghana to see how they could help the cocoa farmers. They looked at all the by-products, things left over after the cocoa beans had been sent to market, and found ways to use these to give more money to the growers.

The cocoa pod used to be wasted, but the project workers found that it could be used as animal feed, called cocoa pod husk feed. They found that they could make potash (originally called potassium carbonate) from the ashes of the cocoa-pod husk and this could be used to make glass and soft soap. They found they could make body creams based on cocoa butter from beans that were rejected as not being good enough to make cocoa or chocolate.

Lucia's parents were now much better off and when Lucia got married to a neighbouring farmer's son, her husband went to live on the farm and soon they had a little girl of their own.

Activities

Ask the children to contrast the lives of Lucia and that of her own daughter after the fair trade co-operative was set up.

In Circle Time, discuss how Lucia would have felt when she realised that her parents and other farmers were being cheated. How would she have felt when the co-operative was formed?

Ask the children to find out about how cocoa beans are grown and how chocolate is made. There are many websites.

Democracy - Reflection

By now, many of the children will have worked with everyone in the class. Discuss how they feel about this and what they have learned from and about other children. Ask them to look through their Global Citizenship folders and read the work they have done about democracy. In Circle Time, discuss what the children now know. What do they remember most about each section?

Talk about how democracy fits into citizenship and whether they think that your classroom is a democratic area.

Have they thought about the effects and the limitations of free speech? If everyone in your classroom said what they thought all the time, would it be a happy place? When reflecting on moral issues, ask the children to consider whether it is ever permissible to tell a lie. On what occasions might it be a kind thing to lie?

When thinking about voting to make things fair for all, can they think of times when someone has to make a decision without a general consensus? Are there occasions when you might think that 'the buck stops here' because a decision has to be made by you, or them? If they have not done so, ask them now to complete the activity sheet 'Democratic or not?'.

Getting involved

Remind the children that this country is a democratic country but that there are many others ruled in different ways. Ask them to think what kinds of things they can do now and in the future to make sure that they are democratic in their dealings with people in the classroom, at home and in their community.

Global challenges

Reflect on the importance of fair trade. Has what they have learned influenced their choice of what they want to buy or even what their parents buy? Will this affect them in the future when they are in control of their own finances? Will they choose to buy, for example, trainers that have been manufactured under fair trade rules? Will they look for the Fairtrade logo and pay a little more to make it fair to the manufacturers of goods?

Rights and responsibilities

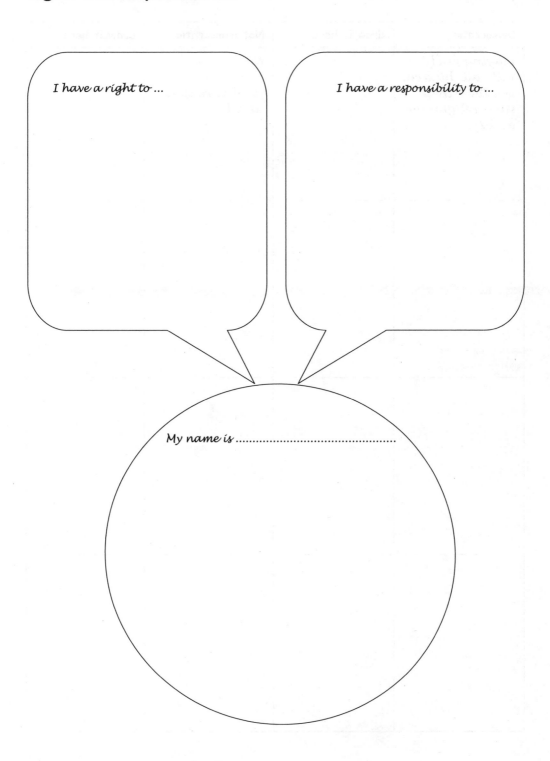

I have a right to ...

I have a responsibility to ...

My name is ....

Democratic or not?

Democratic	draw it here	Not democratic	draw it here
Playing fairly with all children, whatever their race, religion or ability.		*Not letting someone play for any reason at all.*	

A personal budget plan

In the 'Balance' column, write in the amount of money you have now, leaving the other columns blank. When you receive money, write in the date, how much it is and where it is from. Add it to the balance. When you spend money, write the date, how much you spent and what you bought. Take this amount away from the balance, that's the money you should have left.

Date	Income			Expenditure			Balance	
	where from	£.	p.	what bought	£.	p.	£.	p.

My Manifesto

My name is ....

and I think I would make a good representative because ....

....

....

....

....

If you elected me to be the representative, I would ....

....

....

....

....

Section 6

Global issues

Focus

This section is intended to help children to learn about peace and poverty at home or abroad; where we fit into the general pattern and our part in trying to make the world a better place to live in. The first two are not specifically about global issues but set the scene for the following? In particular the children will be exploring the notions of:

peace at school and home
quarrels
peace in this country
wars
world peace
poverty, nationally and worldwide
disasters, at home and abroad.

Remind the children to keep their Global Citizenship folder up to date by putting into it any work they do in this section and to seek out and work with those children they haven't yet worked with.

See the activity sheets at the end of this section: 'Feelings words', 'Better or worse?', 'A fresh new world', 'Who helps?' and 'Can you help?'

You may find the following websites informative:

www.oxfam.org.uk
www.peacecorps.gov
www.savethechildren.org.uk
www.unicef.org.uk
www.worldvision.org.uk

Global issues – younger children

Peace at school and home

Start by reading either *Peace at Last* or *Five Minutes' Peace*, both by Jill Murphy. Explain that peace means harmony, getting on with something and not bothering someone. The opposite of peace is war, but at home the opposite of peace is conflict or quarrels. Ask them to draw a picture of someone having five minutes' peace and to write about their picture.

Ask the children to think about how they feel when there is peace and to tell you words that explain these feelings. Write them up under a heading 'peaceful feelings'. Ask the children to think of the opposite of this kind of peace and make a second list of words that tell about those feelings, such as hot, angry, fed up, worried, anxious.

In Circle Time, talk about times at school when everything goes well and it is peaceful. Ask them to think of what things happen to cause this and to finish the sentence:

I give my Dad five minutes' peace.

'I feel peaceful at school when ...'

Talk about peace at home and what kinds of things happen there to make it a peaceful place. Ask them to finish the sentence:

'It's peaceful at home when ...'

Have they blamed other people for the lack of peace, for messing around or spoiling things? Have they thought of their own actions?

Ask each child to write a 'feelings' word in a daisy on the 'Feelings words' activity sheet at the end of this section. In Circle Time, put them in a pile in the middle; ask each child in turn to take one word and say whether it is a 'good feeling' to cut out to make into a garden picture or a 'not good feeling' to throw in the bin.

Explain that we must take some responsibility for peace at home and at school. It will help if we can keep these good feelings and get rid of the others. Let's try to think of other people, how they are feeling and what they need. It's when we think of what we want all the time and forget other people that things get tense and people get angry. People who think of themselves all the time are not usually peaceful people.

Global issues – older children

Peace at school and home

You could use the daisy on the 'Feelings words' activity sheet with younger children as outlined on the opposite page, or ask older children to draw their own flower with space for a feelings word. Bad feelings words are weeds to be destroyed.

Ask each child to make a list of words that mean the same as peace. Discuss each word, its exact meaning and whether it does mean the same as peace.

Ask the children to work in pairs or small groups to make a list of all the things that make school a peaceful and productive place. Ask each group to join with another group and merge their list to make one. Do this again and again until you end up with just one list. Talk about the children's responsibility in doing these things to make and keep your classroom a peaceful and harmonious place. Can they see that it is in their hands and that their behaviour affects the harmony of your classroom?

Ask the children to decide which of these statements is correct.

If you're always peaceful you're a wimp who doesn't do anything useful.
If you're always peaceful you're nice to be with and a good friend.

Ask them to vote on which they think is true and to get together to prepare a discussion on that statement. Organise a debate. Does one side win? Do they agree to differ? Do they think that circumstances could make either true? Can they amend one of the statements to make it more true?

Ask the children to think of the things they do that help to make and keep their home a peaceful or not peaceful place. Ask them to make two lists and share these lists with a friend. Ask volunteers to share their list with the class. Ask them all to think of a time they caused peace to be shattered. What did they do? How did the situation end? Ask them to draw a picture of this happening, and write about why they shattered the peace and what happened.

Learning at home

Ask the children to think of the last time they resolved a conflict situation at home or outside school and made peace. Ask them to write about what happened, how they felt and how other people felt.

Global issues – younger children

Quarrels

In Circle Time, ask the children to tell you why they think that children quarrel. Ask them to finish the sentence:

'I think children quarrel because ...'

Make a list of what they say and talk about each one.

Talk about quarrels getting out of hand and leading to physical hurt – can they tell you why this happens? Do they know it's sometimes because they haven't the words to explain their side and feel the need to hit out? What sort of things can children do to stop this? Make a list of what they say. Have they included counting to ten, stopping and thinking, thinking about how the other person would feel?

Children quarrel because they ...
want to be first
want something
think they are best
want their own way
want to be the leader
only think of themselves
are unhappy
want to fight.

Talk about the importance of making up quarrels and say that we know this is not easy. Ask them to think about the kinds of things children can do and say to make up after a quarrel and ask them to finish this sentence:

'To make up after I quarrel I could ...'

List all the good ideas and talk about them. Which is the best? Which is the worst? Can you rate the list? Using the idea from the activity sheet 'Better or Worse?,' help the children to make pairs of words. Write them on the board. Make cards using the words and use them to play the games suggested in the activity sheet.

Talk about other quarrels, those between grown-ups. Explain that when grown-ups quarrel it is never the fault of their children. Do they think their ideas of how children can make up after a quarrel could work with grown-ups? What kinds of things do grown-ups do to make up after a quarrel? Do these always work? Talk about quarrels between adults and children. It is not always the child's fault when grown-ups are cross with them but it always helps if the child says they are sorry for something they have done wrong or for any mistake they have made.

Talk about saying 'sorry'. Sometimes this is very hard to do. It's even harder sometimes to mean 'sorry'. Can the children suggest ways they can show they are truly sorry? What kinds of things can they do to show this?

Global issues – older children

Quarrels

Tell the children you want to explore with them the reasons why children quarrel. Ask them each to draw two people of their age quarrelling and to write about what they are doing and saying. Ask them to think about the feelings of the two children they have drawn and to write down how both children feel. Ask them to change papers with a partner, to read that paper and to write a list of what each child could do to end the quarrel. Come together as a class and talk about these quarrels and the suggested ways to resolve them.

Ask the children to think back to a quarrel they had with someone. Give them time to reflect on why the quarrel occurred, whose fault it was and the kinds of things each person said and did. Ask them to work in pairs and to take turns to talk about their quarrels. Ask them to try to answer these questions:

Was quarrelling the right thing to do in those circumstances?
Could you have done something else instead of quarrelling?
What could you have done? List these.
What was the outcome of the quarrel?
Was it a good outcome for either of them or only one of them?
How did both people feel after the quarrel?
With hindsight, can they think of another way to act instead of quarrelling?

Talk about how grown-ups resolve differences. Everyone can't have their own way and sometimes they have to compromise. Make sure they know what 'compromise' means by asking volunteers to say what they think, for example, co-operate, find a middle ground, give and take.

Remind them of the section on voting; this is sometimes a good way to solve a difference of opinion. Remind them that getting angry and losing one's temper is not a good way. Can the children see that peace between nations might be obtained if nations sought ways to resolve their differences?

Learning at home

Write a story about two people who had a quarrel, how it started, what the people said and did and how it was resolved in the end. Can they make their own 'Better or Worse' cards from the activity sheet idea to play with at home?

Global issues – younger children

Peace in this country

Remind the children that this country is a democracy and that the people in it all have equal rights. Remind them that grown-ups all have a vote to decide the government of this country. This should mean that all is peaceful but they know that it is not.

People in this country do not all live in peace and harmony; there are many people who are fighting against the rules and trying to draw other people into their fights. Explain that just as quarrels between children cause anger and worry, so quarrels between groups of grown-ups can grow to cause upset and danger to everyone.

Ask the children if they can think of the kinds of things that grown-ups get angry about. Make a list and talk about what is on it. Do people get angry because they want things to change and would changes be for the better? Do the people get angry with the government because they want money to be spent in a different way? How do people show they are angry and want things to change? Ask the children to tell you what they know.

Talk about what people can do to get good changes and have a more peaceful life. Talk about what people do to try to make others listen, such as sign petitions, go on demonstrations, not pay council tax, write to the papers, vote differently. Which of these are peaceful ways?

Ask the children to think about people who fight in this country for other reasons; can they tell you any? For example, because they have drunk too much alcohol, have taken drugs, are against other races or religions, don't like their neighbours, feel wild and angry, because they are terrorists.

People want ...
to earn more money
to pay less tax
more hospitals
more doctors
cheaper houses
better food
new schools
better roads
no graffiti
no fighting
no drugs

Remind the children that the police are there to enforce law and order and to keep this country a safe and peaceful place.

Global issues – older children

Peace in this country

Bring in some local and national newspapers of recent dates.

Remind the children that quarrels can lead to conflict; discuss anything in your school or community that has led to conflict recently.

Share pages of the local newspapers and ask the children to work in pairs or small groups to identify some cases where there has been conflict. Ask the children to cut out or copy their findings.

As a whole class, talk about whether these conflicts are positive or negative; whether people are trying to fight for people's rights or for a better environment or whether people are in conflict or fighting because they are anti-social, acting against the law or trying to bully others.

Separate the cuttings into two sets, positive conflict and negative conflict, and paste them onto two different pieces of paper with space around them for more work.

Ask the children to work in pairs and choose one of the positive items to discuss. Ask them to think about how the occurrence started, whether it was someone's fault, the action that people are taking and whether they can identify any resolution. Ask them to write their ideas. If several children have selected the same item, ask them to get together to amalgamate their ideas; discuss these and paste them alongside the newspaper cuttings.

Ask the children to do the same exercise with one of the negative cuttings.

Write the following so that children can choose which statement they think is correct.

> *It's always OK to fight for your rights. It's not always OK to fight for your rights.*

Ask each side to prepare for a discussion, choose a spokesperson and debate.

Learning at home

Ask the children to research past conflicts when people were fighting for their rights, either in this country or in other countries. They can use their families, friends, books and the Internet. Ask them to write a short piece in three sections, the causes, the action and the results.

Global issues – younger children

Wars

Explain to young children that just as people quarrel, so do countries, and that wars between countries have been going on for a very long time.

Explain that each country has a fighting force to protect the people of that country against people who might want to harm them. Talk about the Navy, the Army and the Air Force as the forces that guard and protect us against war. Ask them to tell you if any of their parents or relatives have ever been in the forces.

Explain that this country hasn't been invaded since 1066 but that the people have been involved in wars in other countries. Talk about World War II and how people in this country had to go to war on foreign soil to stop aggression in other countries before their troops could invade us. If you have touched on World War II in your studies, remind the children about what the people in this country had to do to survive the bombing, the Blitz and the deprivations of food and energy that were inevitable in wartime. Ask them to tell you what they know from what their grandparents and great-grandparents have told them about that war. Ask them to draw a picture of someone in their family who went to war and to say which of the forces this person was in.

My Grandad drove an armoured car in Northern Ireland.

Explain that this country belongs to an organisation called the United Nations, the UN, a kind of friendship group, that calls upon the people of the member countries to send help to other countries where there is conflict. The UN doesn't only send forces to help against aggression; it sends aid, food, doctors, nurses and medical supplies to help the people who need these things.

Talk about the ideals of soldiers going to fight for their country. Talk about combat games that children play. Do they think it's good to play wars? Do they know that some grown-ups play war games, sometimes dressing up in old uniforms and acting out battles? In these play battles no-one is killed; it is not the same in real wars.

Global issues – older children

Wars

Write up the following sentences for discussion:

"War is never a good thing; I would never want to fight."

"Sometimes countries have to fight wars. I would fight in the right cause."

Ask the children to choose which they think is correct and to form two debating groups. (You may like to sub-divide into smaller groups.) Give them time to write down their arguments in favour of their chosen sentence before debating the issues. At the end, ask them to vote to choose which they think is correct.

You will have talked about World War II in your studies and the children will have some idea of the battles fought in order to prevent invasion of this country. In Circle Time, arrange a discussion about the rights and wrongs of that war. With hindsight, can any of them suggest a different route? What might have been the consequences?

Talk with the children about the kinds of issues that could make war acceptable, for example, stopping oppression, stopping 'ethnic cleansing', to help citizens of countries where there is no democracy.

Can the children think of alternatives to war in the cases they describe? If so, list these alternatives and discuss possible outcomes.

The United Nations (UN) is an organisation formed in 1948. In the words of its Charter, it was formed in order 'to save succeeding generations from the scourge of war'. It now has 192 member states. One of its aims is about missions for peace, but unfortunately in order to do this it sends peacekeeping troops into countries where there is conflict; in other words, sometimes it has to fight for peace.

Learning at home

Use the Internet to find out about the United Nations, its aims and peacekeeping responsibilities. Explore its other missions, for example, humanitarian. Discuss the children's findings and from these write a class mission statement to describe the work of the UN to put in their folders.

Global issues – younger children

World peace

Talk to the children about peace in the whole world. Explain that there are several organisations that promote world peace but that this doesn't happen. Remind them how difficult it is to be peaceful at home and in the classroom and explain that in the whole world this becomes even more difficult.

Ask the children to think what kinds of things could help to make the world a peaceful place. Ask them to finish the sentence:

'The world would be more peaceful if ...'

Make a list of what the children say, discuss each one and help them to add more to the list.

Write the word 'peace' on the board. Talk about colour, shape and form and ask the children to close their eyes and think what a picture of 'peace' might look like. Ask them to make a picture of peace using any media: paint, pastel, crayon, collage. Talk about their various ideas before mounting and displaying their pictures. Add speech bubbles of what they told you about the world being more peaceful.

> *The world would be more peaceful if*
>
> *people stopped quarrelling*
> *things were fairer*
> *everyone was more friendly*
> *people helped each other*
> *things were shared out*
> *everyone respected each other*
> *we loved all our neighbours.*

Examine the wall pictures and read the speech bubbles with the children. Ask the children to help you to write a poem about peace. You could write a haiku – a short poem in three lines with five syllables in the first and last line and seven for the middle line, for example:

Everyone wants peace
An end to war and fighting
Peace for everyone.

Ask older children to write their own haiku, free or rhyming verse. Explain that what it says is more important that whether it has a rhythm.

Explain that world peace must start with individual people feeling peaceful towards and love for other people. Organise a pair, group and a class hug.

Global issues – older children

World peace

Read through the work for younger children and use what is appropriate with your class. Ask the children to work in pairs to find synonyms and antonyms in words or phrases of the word 'peace'. Share these to make one set for a display later.

Ask the children to think of the work they have already done in this section and to work in pairs to list the reasons why countries go to war. Share this work with another pair and then another four before coming together as a class to make one list. Look at the kinds of words and phrases that the children have used, for example, oppression, fighting, greed, racial tension. Ask them to find opposites to these words and make these into positive terms, for example, oppression might become liberty, fighting become discussion, greed become giving and racial tension become acceptance. Make a list of these words.

Ask the children to think of a design or logo that your class could use to promote world peace. Ask them to work in pairs and to use various media to produce their design. Ask them to choose one or more of the positive words or phrases on their list above and to integrate this into their logo.

Display their logos surrounded by peaceful words written in peaceful colours on white clouds. Add spiky warlike words banished in the distance in black clouds. Ask them to complete the activity sheet 'A fresh new world'. Share their ideas of what would make a new world a happy place for every one.

Ask them to think about how world peace might come about. What kind of people could make it happen? How could they do it? Will it ever come about?

Learning at home

Challenge the children to find out about organisations that are working towards world peace and to list these for discussion at school the next day.

Ask each child to think about how a nation would feel when peace is declared after a long war. Ask them to make a list of these words and to write a story about how a family would feel when there was peace again in their world.

Global issues – younger children

Poverty, nationally and worldwide

Ask the children to draw a picture of someone who is poor. Share their pictures and talk about each one.

Now ask them what they think 'poor' means using the finish the sentence technique:

'I think poor means ...'

Make a note of what they say and talk about any misconceptions. Explain that we use the word 'poor' to mean all kinds of things that don't mean lacking in resources. Look again at their pictures; did any draw someone poor?

A poor old woman lived in a shoe.

Ask them if they know anyone who is really poor – someone who is hungry without enough to eat, or with nowhere to live, or no decent clothes to wear. Explain that there are not as many really poor people in this country as there are in other countries but that there are some people who do not have enough money to buy the things they really need.

Explain that in this country the government normally makes sure that people who are really poor are helped by giving them extra money or by finding places for them to live but that there are still some people with nowhere to live who can't get this extra money because they have no address.

Ask the children to tell you how they think it would feel to be really hungry and to have no food or nowhere to live.

Explain that in other countries there are many children whose parents and families have died who are really poor. Some children are starving and some live on the streets just picking up what food they can and sleeping in doorways. Tell them that there are good people who are trying to help these children but that it is not easy because there are so many of them.

Talk about the charities with people who work to help poor children around the world by sending money, clothes or food. Do they know the names of any of these charities? Make a list of them. Do they sometimes put money in collecting boxes to help them? Could you organise a collection?

Global issues – older children

Poverty, nationally and worldwide

Talk to the children about poverty. Ask them to tell you what they know about people, living in this country, who are poor, for example, sellers of *The Big Issue*, people living in doorways, shelters for the homeless.

Discuss how people become homeless, for example, runaways, people whose marriages have broken up, homes lost through lack of income. Explain that the government helps by trying to find bed and breakfast accommodation and giving extra benefit to homeless people but that sometimes people do not qualify for benefit and relief.

Ask the children to write a few sentences to describe how they would feel if something happened to them and they were suddenly without family or home. Ask them to think about the kinds of things they would miss. What could they do?

Ask the children to discuss the following statements from the Save the Children website:

> The majority of poor people in the world are children. Their lack of income and access to other resources means that they can't ensure the basics of life like food, good health, education and housing. The extent and severity of global poverty are directly linked to economic policies and activities that ignore children's right to a happy, healthy and secure childhood.

Explain that some of the richer countries have organisations that try to help people in the developing countries but that this isn't easy because sometimes the help they try to give goes to the wrong people. Can they give you the names of some of these agencies? Ask them to work in pairs to compile a list of the kinds of help that richer countries could give. How do they think people in the poorer countries feel about this kind of help?

Learning at home

Ask the children to find out from the Internet about one of the agencies that try to help children in other countries. What are its aims? Which countries does it help? How does it make sure that aid gets to the people who need it most? Ask them to write about how young people, such as themselves, could help.

Global issues – younger children

Disasters, at home and abroad

Talk with the children about the word 'disaster'. Do people use this word when they just mean that something has gone wrong? Ask them to finish the sentence:

It was a disaster when our kitchen flooded.

'It was a disaster when …'

Talk about what happened to put this 'disaster' right – who helped and what did they do?

Explain that the disasters you are talking about are more serious than that and remind the children about any recent disasters in your area, such as flooding, fires or accidents. Talk about whether these could have been prevented or whether they are natural disasters where the cause was out of our hands.

Make two lists on your board under the headings 'natural disasters', 'man-made disasters' and talk about each one.

Who helped in these disasters? Talk about the agencies that are there to help communities when things go wrong. Make a list of them, starting with the fire service. Read through your list and decide which are run by people who are paid to do that work and which are manned by volunteers. Talk about the kind of people who volunteer to help in emergencies and that lifeboat crews, for example, are released from their paid work immediately they hear the alarm call for them to go and man the lifeboat. Explain that these volunteers are really committed citizens who often put their own lives at risk to help others.

Ask the children to think of any local disasters, either from memory or by looking through local newspapers. Ask them to determine the cause and effect of that disaster. Ask them to write down all that people did to help when that disaster struck. Talk about any current disasters in the wider world. Who are the people helping here and what are they doing to help? Do people in this country send aid? What kind of aid and how do they do it?

Global issues – older children

Disasters, at home and abroad

Read through the activities for younger children and discuss any that are appropriate.

Ask the children to work in pairs to make two lists. natural disasters, such as earthquakes, man-made disasters, such as war. Ask one pair to share their list with the whole group and ask other pairs to add theirs until you end up with one pair of complete lists.

Talk about what we can do to help in the event of a natural disaster. Remind the children of the most recent one, how the world heard about it and what other nations did to help.

Discuss the kinds of people who go to help in these extreme disasters; are they all specialists in what is needed or are some volunteers who go to do anything they can to help? Discuss the kinds of help that people who cannot travel to help directly can give.

Talk about man-made disasters in the past, such as ethnic cleansing, the Holocaust, oil spillage, shipwrecks and talk about what other nations of the world did to help. Discuss whether peacekeeping or other troops were sent in and whether this was the best option. What were the other options? Which nations sent help?

Discuss the AIDS/HIV epidemic in all countries and what is being done to help people in developing countries where this is rife. Are they getting the aid they require? Who is sending it? Ask the children to do the activity sheets 'Who helps?' and 'Can you help?' at the end of this section.

Learning at home

Ask the children to select one disaster to investigate; it could be a current or past disaster. Ask them to write a report about it for a fictional newspaper. Share their work in Circle Time and discuss the implications. You could then make a display of their writing with artwork under the title 'Disasters'.

Shuralina's story

Shuralina lived in a small fishing village on the edge of the Indian Ocean. Her father was a fisherman and her oldest brother, who was 17, helped. Her two younger brothers helped with the nets and the fish sometimes after school was over but Shuralina was the youngest at six years old and because she was a girl she didn't help with the fishing work; she helped her mother in the house.

They were a very happy family living almost on the shoreline. They had a small house made of concrete blocks and wood with windows overlooking the sea. They didn't have a garden, but the area outside their home was used for spreading the nets and mending them and for berthing the fishing boat when it was not out on the sea.

Very rarely, only on high days and holidays, the whole family would go out in the fishing boat to sail around the shore. They would take a picnic and spend the day together, waving and smiling at other families who would do the same. Shuralina enjoyed these rare days; her brothers were fun when they were not working and they teased her in a kind way and made her feel special.

Behind the houses of the fisherfolk there were some small hotels because tourists liked to visit their village. Tourists liked the sunshine and lazed about around the large swimming pools when they were there on holiday. Shuralina's father sold most of his fish to one particular hotel. The chef there made sure he had a fair price for his fish and so the little family had a good life with enough to eat, enough clothes to wear and enough toys to play with.

At school Shuralina was already learning to speak English. This was the language of the American tourists and most other tourists spoke English as well as their own language. Sometimes she would go with her father when he delivered the fish and try to speak a little English to the children she saw in the hotel grounds.

The tourists would walk along the beach and peer at the fishing boats and look at the houses of the fishermen's families. The tourists would think that these homes were quaint because they were very small and didn't have all the facilities in their own homes. Some of them pitied the fishermen's families because they thought they didn't have modern houses, clothes, cars and machines. Shuralina couldn't understand this because she thought that she had everything she could want; a loving family, plenty to eat, even if a lot of it was fish, a few books and a good school to go to.

It was a very peaceful life for Shuralina and her family, although sometimes they worried if the sea came up a bit too high and lapped against their front door. Shuralina's father would watch the sea anxiously in case it rose and came inside the house but it had never done that.

Then one day something dreadful happened. Shuralina's father and oldest brother were out fishing and she was sitting outside the doorway helping to prepare vegetables for their supper when she noticed that the sea seemed to be high in the distance. She watched as a great wave came nearer and nearer and then ran inside the house to tell her mother and two brothers. They rushed outside to see it; it was huge! They looked for a minute and then Shuralina's mother said, 'Quick, quick, we must run for shelter, it's coming in and will wash us all away'. She grabbed Shuralina's hand and pushed the two brothers in front of her and they began to run inland and upwards, away from the tidal wave. Before they had gone far they looked back and saw a huge wall of water coming right at them. 'Run, run, find somewhere to shelter', shouted their mother as she dragged Shuralina up the hill.

The water didn't stop. It surged around their feet, knocked them over and they were all being pushed about. Houses were falling, cars were floating, people everywhere were shouting and calling for help. Shuralina was knocked into a wall; her head banged into the concrete and everything went black.

She awoke slowly and opened her eyes. She was lying on a wet mattress and someone was leaning over her. It was one of the tourists, who shouted, 'She's waking, I think she's OK, just a bump on her head really, come and look.' A woman came to look. 'You were lucky!' she said, 'your legs are bleeding but nothing's broken but I think we'll take you to see the doctor anyway'.

Shuralina felt bruised and battered but the cuts on her legs were not too bad. She felt her head and there was a large bump. Then she remembered. Where was her mother? Where were her brothers? What about her father and oldest brother in their fishing boat?

In the hospital she was given food and her legs were treated. Her name was posted up as a survivor and people she didn't know came to talk to her to ask her where she had lived and about her family. There were lots of people she didn't know; some were tourists from the hotel high on the hill, others were rescuers who had come from other areas of her country or from far away to help in the disaster.

The next day she went to see her home. There was nothing there; everything had been washed away; she couldn't recognise anywhere as it was all changed. None of Shurina's family had survived. Her father and brother had been washed out to sea and were never seen again. Her mother and two brothers had been killed in the flood. Shuralina was all alone.

Activities

Do you think it was fair that Shuralina wasn't allowed to help with the fishing work? Is this a gender problem or do you think that she might have preferred to work with her mother in the house? Draw a picture of Shuralina and her home and family. Imagine that you were part of her family, a brother or sister, and write how you would have felt living that kind of life.

Why do you think that Shuralina and her friends wanted to learn to speak English? What other languages would be as useful to her?

Shuralina thought she was lucky because of the things she had in her life. Make a list of the essential things in your life and why you think these things on your list are important. Would they be important to all children in your class?

How do you think Shuralina felt as she was being swept away in the flood? How do you think she felt when she was rescued and taken to hospital? How would she feel when she realised that all her family had gone? Make a list of all the feelings you think she would have had.

Write your own ending to Shuralina's story.

Global Issues – Reflection

Ask the children to look at their list of children they have worked with. Encourage those who have a short list to find ways to work with those not yet on their list. Explain that this will give them a true understanding of inclusion.

Ask them to read through their folders, making sure they add copies of any displayed work. Discuss what the children now know and what they remember most about each of the sections. Ask them to reflect on how peace at home and school and avoiding or resolving quarrels are, in their small way, important steps in avoiding global unrest.

Explain to the children that in the future it will be their generation that rules the country and that they must try to work towards world peace and not war. Remind them that war destroys; not only people's lives but also their heritage, beautiful buildings, books, traditions and their ways of living. Remind them that, over centuries, many people fleeing persecution have been accepted into this country and granted citizenship with its rights and responsibilities.

Remind the children of the work they did about poverty, explaining that many children in poorer countries are just as happy as children in this country; in fact some may well be happier because they are content with their pleasures and are not greedy in demanding others. Children from far away have much to teach us about living a good and useful life and we must be careful not to pity or patronise them because of the things they do not have or the ways they live.

Getting involved

Remind the children that because we belong to a rich nation we have a responsibility to help nations that are still developing. Challenge them to remember this and to do all they can to help or persuade others to help.

Global challenges

There are few things that children can do to help children in other countries but a lot they can do to help people from different backgrounds who live here. A positive challenge is to remember that all people are equal; whatever their background or ability they are members of mankind; as such they are brothers and sisters.

Fact sheet: extracts from a 'Save the Children' promotion circular, September 2006

43 million children growing up in war zones around the world are missing out on school, which means they'll be more likely to become child soldiers, more likely to be shot or blown up by a landmine, more likely to be raped or sexually exploited and end up with AIDS. And if they survive all this, they'll be more likely to grow up poor and die young.

In war torn countries like Sudan, Uganda and Nepal there's often no choice (for children to go to school) ... schools are destroyed and teachers killed ... pens, paper and chalk may be almost impossible to get hold of ... classes may have 200 children in them taught by a teacher who's never had a day's training.

In Southern Sudan, just 20% of children enrol in primary school – and only 2% finish it.

Selestina (Angola) is a bright girl who should ... go far. But she spent much of her childhood hiding from soldiers who might rape, abduct or jail her. So her education is very behind.

Sifa (Democratic Republic of Congo) says 'There is no money for my food, clothes and to go to school. That is why it isn't possible to go to school right now.'

War destroys; education rebuilds.

see www.savethechildren.org.u/rewritethefuture to find out more.

Feelings words

Write a feelings word in the centre of the flower. Cut out your daisy.

Better or worse?

Think of what you do that can make things better or worse when there is a quarrel or conflict. Write pairs of words in these boxes.

Better	Worse	Better	Worse
keeping calm	shouting		
being in control	being angry		
listening	not listening		

Using words from all the children, ask them to make several sets of cards to use in the following games:

1. In Circle Time, shuffle the cards and give each person one. Ask each child in turn to stand up and read their card. Ask the person with the opposite to stand and read theirs; when correct they sit together with their pair of cards.
2. Shuffle and deal the cards to four people. Each child asks the next if they have the opposite of their word, collecting cards if they have one. The winner is the one with the most cards.
3. Place all cards face down and ask four children to pick up and memorise a card each turn. When they can find a pair of opposites they collect that pair.

A fresh new world

Imagine a fresh new world being created ...

Draw a map or globe of this world.

Draw some of the different-coloured people in this fresh new world.

This new world is a happy, safe place for everyone.

Think of the things that the people who live in this happy new world will have. Write them here.

What kinds of things, feelings or attitudes will there **never** be in this fresh new world? Write them here.

Who helps? What can they do?

Think of all the people who help in emergencies, tragedies and disasters both at home and abroad. Write their names on the left and what they do on the right. If you can think of more, turn over the paper and use the other side.

The Red Cross	

Can you help?

What could you do? Write a letter to a friend, saying what you could do for people who need help in another country. Use the other side of the paper if you need more room.

.... school

.... date

Dear ....

Appendix

Milford on Sea C of E Primary School, Hampshire: A Case Study in Global Citizenship

Written by Frances Hillier, April 2006.

Formerly Education Adviser to Link Community Development and currently Assistant Project Officer for LCD Malawi.

All the children made tiles for this picture

'Far round the world thy children sing their song;
From East and West their voices sweetly blend,
Praising the Lord in whom young lives are strong,
Jesus our guide, our hero and our friend.

When Basil Mathews, 1879-1951, wrote this children's hymn with its global and missionary theme, he can hardly have known how those 'young lives' would change in the next few decades. His passion and concern for making children in the UK more aware of their brothers and sisters overseas, was reflected in magazines he edited called *Far Horizons* and *News from Afar*.

Now with the Internet, electronic encyclopedias and state of the art computer suites, children on the northern side of the equator have indeed got easy access to far horizons and news from all over the global village.

But what about their peers to the south of that invisible dividing line? Just how much real contact can exist between children who, as the Head Teacher, Martin Pitman, said are 'fundamentally the same, though culturally different'?

Here at Milford-on-Sea Church of England Primary School, a few miles outside Southampton, every effort is made to enhance the pupils' awareness of their own good fortune and to help them become responsible global citizens. Opportunities abound both within and around the curriculum to promote knowledge, skills and attitudes that celebrate differences and recognise similarities. Having an ethos within the Christian tradition gives the children strong links with adults connected to their church who are working overseas.

They learn directly from people such as Toox, the church's Ugandan missionary nurse and Geoff Hill, the family worker who has visited India and brought the pastor from their linked church to visit the school. Geoff has also shown photos of children in the Indian community in school which has brought a sense of immediacy and context to the work he does. The vicar's son has recently returned from Rwanda and gave a talk to several classes. Having a school governor who is from South Africa is another valued component of the global jigsaw and brings home the wide range of cultures and backgrounds that may be unknown to many living in the virtual mono-culture in this quiet haven in southern England.

Library books and videos, DVDs and CD-ROMs are readily available both at the school and in the pupils' homes – the global village at the touch of a button – but what can deepen the visual and aural impact of such tools, to touch emotions and strengthen attitudes such as empathy?

A group of articulate 11-year-old members of the School Council were keen to talk about activities they had participated in which had had such an effect.

Pictures such as this became a living reality when the staff organised a 'Water Aid' fund-raising day. Some of the children walked round and round the playing field carrying buckets of water. It was their arms, rather than their necks that got tired, but the impact was imprinted in muscles as well as in minds. Water from rivers is often unclean, yet all that effort goes into collecting it every single day and children their age get sick and die from water-borne diseases. The money they raised will go towards providing the means to prevent such inequalities.

Another 'moving' experience came through the visit of an Indian dance expert, Shushmita. Learning about the meaning of the movements they were asked to copy, as well as watching the graceful performer, gave greater insight into another culture. Religious symbolism and beliefs were shared together with music and dance. A study of India is already embedded in the Geography curriculum for Year 5 and so the pages of the textbooks and the flat maps in the atlas begin to take on another dimension and acquire a new life which involves real people doing real things.

Music is a strong medium for registering emotions and motivating memory. A gamelan workshop introduces a whole new complex culture of sounds: sounds of mystery from far away, from the islands of Indonesia such as Java and Bali. The wide range of unfamiliar and more recognisable instruments gives new opportunities to ask questions and go back to the atlas to ask 'Where in the world …?'

As indeed does Barnaby Bear (a registered trademark of the Geographical Association) who goes on his travels and takes the youngest children to many different parts of the world.

Citizenship and its associated values and perceptions is just one aspect of developing a global dimension to every area of this school's life. Social justice, human rights, conflict resolution, sustainable development, diversity and interdependence are all interlocking concepts that contribute to a community that is sensitive to the needs of the planet and its people.

Many children at Milford C of E Primary will be able to make informed comments on why it is better to recycle as much household waste as possible *and* what Christian Aid means when they urge us to 'recycle a goat'. (www.christianaid.org.uk). Sending a cow to Africa had an impact on some of the School Council and they reflected on several ways in which such a gift benefited the lady who received it and wrote to say 'thank you'. While fund-raising for current emergencies and sending shoe boxes of toys each Christmas is a constant part of the ethos of this school, there is also the deeper level of engagement with the reasons and impact of showing concern for 'those who are less fortunate than us'.

Assemblies for pupils and their parents address issues such as Fair Trade and Global Warming. A travelling theatre was invited to share their production about energy-saving in the home and staff and other adults have recounted stories and shown photos of their experiences in places such as Lagos, as a thriving modern city and not the stereotypical image of mud huts and poverty. Children's passion for games and sports can also provide a rich seam of thought provoking questions on the justice of child-labour issues involved in making cricket balls and trainers.

The banana leaf collage of boys playing football that stands on the beautifully arranged table in the entrance hall speaks volumes about the values placed on the school's contacts with other countries and cultures. What is their football made of?

Growing seeds as a sponsored activity has made children more aware of both how their own food is grown as well as researching where the goods on the supermarket shelves come from. Food miles, sustainable development and the injustice of the hunger experienced by 60 percent or more of their peers in other countries will help these children develop a deeper understanding of the inter-related issues of how they can vote with their pocket money as well as their feet.

Putting yourself in someone else's shoes is a familiar metaphor for developing empathy, tolerance and understanding. How giant a leap is it for children in such a well-favoured school as this, to walk in the footsteps of those who have no shoes?

One way is by having a partnership with a specific school.

Link Community Development (LCD) is an International Development agency with a clear vision. Their literature states:

'LCD's vision is of a future where children are given a chance to flourish and fulfil their potential. Our mission is to improve the potential of disadvantaged people in Africa to gain meaningful employment by sharing and developing appropriate skills through education and training. We believe that education is a basic human right and fundamental to breaking the cycle of poverty.

Through our *Link Schools Programme*, UK schools can link with Ghanaian, South African, Ugandan and Malawian schools. Link Community Development runs education development projects in these countries which include over 400 schools. Link sets up the linking, helps facilitate communication and provides the UK school with a detailed profile of the African school, background information, suggestions for development education activities and annual updates from the Link project that your partner school is part of.

A link with an African school can teach UK children about the wider world and help them develop into *Global citizens* who participate in the community at both the local and international level. Not only is this an opportunity for staff and pupils to make lasting friendships, but also to make the curriculum more interesting and immediate. Schools involved in curriculum-related international work can also gain accreditation under the *International School Award Scheme*.

Milford C of E Primary is clearly well along the path of developing Global Citizens. By committing to a partnership with a school on the other side of the world, they may well find that their global world becomes even richer.

With thanks to the Head, staff and pupils of Milford C of E Primary school for their time and co-operation.

Other case studies

Schools in the Link organisation:

http://www.lcd.org.uk/uk/casestudies/preston-saboro.pdf

http://www.lcd.org.uk/uk/casestudies/southfields-nyogbare.pdf

Resources

Storybooks

Andersson, S. (1980) *No Two Zebras are the Same*, Lion Publishing, Tring, UK

Arnott K. (1989) *African Myths and Legends*, OUP.

Goble, P. (1998) *Legend of the White Buffalo Woman*, Geographic Soc.

McCaughrean, G. (2001) *100 World Myths & Legends*, Orion.

Naidoo, B. (1999) *Journey to Jo'burg*, Collins Modern Classics.

Jeffers S. (1993) *Brother Eagle, Sister Sky, A Message from Chief Seattle*, Puffin.

Smith, D. J. (2003) *If the world were a village*, Black, London.

Books for children

Barker, A. (1994) *India*, Worldfocus books Heinemann, Oxford.

Bastyra, J. (1996) *Homeless*, Evans Bros, London (Life files series, other titles in series).

Brown, J. (1998) *Comic Relief*, Heinemann, Oxford.

Burke, P. (1997) *Eastern Europe* from World Fact Files, Macdonald Young Books (other books in this series).

Haughton, E. (2000) *Equality of the Sexes?* Franklin Watts, London.

Khan, E. and Unwin, R. (1997) *Pakistan*, Wayland Publishers, Hove.

Macdonald, F. and Weaver, C. (2003) *Human Rights*, Chrysalis Children's Books, London.

Matthews, J. (1993) *I come from Vietnam*, Aladdin Books Ltd, London.

Simonds, R. (1998) *Stand Up for your Rights*, Peace Child International, Two-Can Publishing Ltd., London.

Stearman, K. (1999) *Women's Rights*, Wayland Publishers, Salop.

Wignall, P. (2000) *Prejudice and Difference*, Heinemann, Oxford.

The Taking Action series includes:

Kozak, M. (1997) *Greenpeace*, Heinemann, Oxford.

Clayton, E. (1997) *Oxfam*, Heinemann, Oxford.

Spilsbury, L. (2000) *NSPCC*, Heinemann, Oxford.

Worldfocus books, published by Heinemann; a series of books about various developing countries, including Bangladesh, Kenya and Brazil.

Heinemann series:

Kadodwala, D. and Gateshill, P. (1995) *Celebrate Hindu Festivals*, Heinemann, Oxford.

Wood, A. (1995) *Celebrate Jewish Festivals*, Heinemann, Oxford.

Knight, K. (1955) *Celebrate Islam Festivals*, Heinemann, Oxford.

Also in series – Christian, Sikh and Buddhist festivals.

Resources

Collins, M. (2001) *Because We're Worth It*, London: Paul Chapman Publishing.

Collins, M. (2002) *Circling Round Citizenship*, London: Paul Chapman Publishing.

Collins, M. (2002) *Because I'm Special*, London: Paul Chapman Publishing.

Collins, M (2004) *Circling Safely*, Paul Chapman Publishing, London.

Collins, M. (2004) *But is it Bullying?* Paul Chapman Publishing, London.

Collins, M. (2007) *Circle Time for the Very Young, 2*nd *edition*, Paul Chapman Publishing, London.

DfEE (2000) *Developing a global dimension in the school curriculum*, ref. DfEE 0115/2000.

Fountain, S. (1994) *Learning Together – global education 4–7*, Cheltenham, Stanley Thornes.

Kerr, D. (1999) *Re-examining citizenship education, the case of England*, NFER, Slough.

Wetton, N. and Collins, M. (2002) *Citizenship – the challenge*, HIT Publications, Liverpool.

Wetton, N. and Collins, M. (2003) *Pictures of Health*, Belair Publications Ltd., Dunstable.

Useful organisations

Association for Citizenship Teaching (ACT)
www.teachingcitizenship.org.uk

Citizenship Foundation
Ferroners House, Shaftesbury Place, Aldersgate St, London EC2Y 8AA,
Tel: 020 7367 0500
www.citfou.org.uk

Council for Education in World Citizenship
14 St Swithin's Lane, London EC4N 8AL
Tel: 020 7929 5090

DfES Citizenship
www.dfes.gov.uk/ciizenship/

Institute for Citizenship
62 Marylebone High Street, London W1M 5HZ
Tel: 020 7935 4777
www.citizen.org.uk

National Healthy Schools Standard
www.wiredforhealth.gov.uk

QCA
83 Piccadilly, London W1J 8QA
www.qca.org.uk/ca/subjects/citizenship

Schools Council UK
57 Etchingham Road, London N3 2EB
Tel: 020 8349 2459
www.schoolcouncils.org

For teaching resources

www.globaldimension.org.uk to download 'Developing the global dimension in the school curriculum' from Global Dimension

Oxfam's Cool Planet – http://www.oxfam.org.uk/coolplanet/index.htm

Global Education Derby – www.globaleducationderby.org.uk

The QCA – http://www.qca.org.uk/7907.html

DFES – http://www.dfes.gov.uk/citizenship/

TeacherNet – http://www.teachernet.gov.uk/citizenship/section.cfm?sectionId=5&hierachy=1.5.

www.globaleducationderby.org.uk/newssummer2005.pdf
Teaching resource for an in-depth critical debate about poverty.

Useful websites

www.makepovertyhistory.org/schools
Part of the Make Poverty History (MPH) official website with resources for schools.

www.whiteband.org
Global Call to Action Against Poverty website..

www.un.org/millenniumgoals
Official UN site about the Millennium Development Goals (MDGs).

www.millenniumcampaign.org
A UN campaign site on the MDGs.

www.millenniumcampaign.org/youth
Interactive youth site about the MDGs.

www.youthoftheworld.net
A site for young people, encouraging them to campaign on the MDGs.

www.sendmyfriend.org
Campaign site about MDG 2 universal primary education) with a useful teachers' section.

www.g8.gov.uk
UK Government official G8 website.

www.unicef.org.uk/c8
Children's version of the G8, run by UNICEF.

www.raisedvoices.net
Testimonies from the Global South on the effects G8 policies have on their lives.

www.oneworldweek.org
Site for the annual One World Week. This year's theme is Promises, Promises, relating to the G8 and the MDGs.

www.globaldimension.org.uk
A site to enable teachers to bring a global perspective to teaching.

www.jubileedebtcampaign.org.uk
Jubilee Debt Campaign.

www.tjm.org.uk
Trade Justice Movement.

www.wdm.org.uk
World Development Movement.

www.liberaljudaism.org
Free downloadable MPH teaching pack with excellent, easy to understand background information plus pupil activities.

www.learningafrica.org.uk
A site that offers support for teachers wishing to explore Africa in the classroom.

www.focusweb.org
Focus on the Global South website.

www.dea.org.uk
Provides links to development education centres around the UK.

www.wiredforhealth.gov.uk
Provides information for delivery of health education in schools.

http://www.dfes.gov.uk/a-z/CITIZENSHIP.html

www.rospa.com

Picture books

For foundation age children to read online and information for age groups: foundation, 5–7, 7–11, help them to visit:
http://www.dfes.gov.uk/citizenship/section.cfm?sectionId=21&hierachy=16.21

Available Now from Lucky Duck!

Circle Time for the Very Young
Second Edition

Margaret Collins
Educational Consultant, Southampton

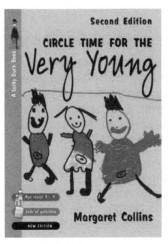

'A fantastic resource for engaging young children in circle time activities...This book will prove to be an invaluable resource for any early years practitioner, whether working in a nursery, playgroup or children's centre' - *Early Years Educator (eye)*

Circle Time is extensively used in primary and increasingly in secondary schools to help young people improve their confidence, speaking and listening skills, and to raise self-esteem. Fully updated and packed with new features such as children's haikus, this new edition is full of brilliant activities for the very young

Contents

Introduction / What You Get in This Book / Framework for Circle Time / The Eight PSHE Themes / Friends and Friendship / Growing and Growing Up / Keeping Safe / Self-Esteem / Keeping Healthy / Feelings and Persuasion / Citizenship / Loss, Grief and Separation / Resources

April 2007 • 160 pages

Paperback (978-1-4129-3030-7) £16.99

www.luckyduck.co.uk
www.paulchapmanpublishing.co.uk PCP

Available Now from Lucky Duck!

Write Dance in the Nursery
A Pre-Writing Programme for Children 3-5

Includes CD-Rom

Ragnhild Oussoren

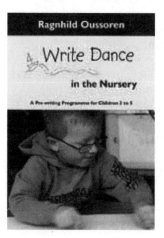

'The Write Dance materials are wonderfully done. After meeting with Ragnhild a few years ago, I have been using many of these principles in my work with children. The methods definitely work and are definitely needed by today's kids' - **Delina Robair, Developmental Child Specialist, USA**

Write Dance is an innovative and exciting programme, widely used across Europe as a way of introducing handwriting using music, movement and exercise. It has been found especially helpful for children with special educational needs, from learning difficulties to dyspraxia.

Contents
What is Write Dance\Toddler-Write Dance\Movements in your space\Movements on a writing surface\Both hands\Consolidating\Experiencing and emotions\Repetition and routine\ Development\Scrimbling area\Materials for the writing surface\Writing materials\Materials for theme play\The role of the teacher\A ten-steps working method for Toddler-Write Dance\Stories\ Movements\ Theme play\ Scrimbling

October 2005 ● 128 pages

Paperback (978-1-4129-1904-3) £25.99 ● Hardcover (978-1-4129-2172-5) £79.00

www.luckyduck.co.uk
www.paulchapmanpublishing.co.uk PCP

Available Now from Lucky Duck!

Creative Circle Time for Early Years

Includes CD-Rom

Yvonne Weatherhead

This creative book uses music, song, poetry and a host of practical ideas to engage children in Circle Time activities. The publication stems from Yvonne's own work in schools where 26 alphabetical themes have been centralised around a lovable bear character.

As an experienced teacher Yvonne offers not only a comprehensive practical resource that all teachers will find useful and time saving, but she also provides links to Citizenship, planning sheets for PSHE, lesson objectives and full lesson notes, providing all the support busy teachers need.

Contents
How to use this book / Typical Circle Time Activities / Useful tips on how to perform a Circle Time lesson / How to develop materials further / Dream Journeys in Foundation Stage and Key Stage One / Circle Time planning linked to Citizenship – Foundation Stage to Year 2 / Lesson Objectives linked to strands of Self-Esteem/Relationships/Communication and Spiritual and Moral Development / Introducing Creative Circle Time (Teacher Script) / Alphabetical bear game / Lessons A-Z / Knitting Pattern

October 2008 ● 150 pages

Paperback (978-1-4129-3533-3) £29.99

www.luckyduck.co.uk

www.paulchapmanpublishing.co.uk PCP